Greg Byrd, Lynn Byrd and Chris Pearce

Cambridge Checkpoint

Mathematics

Skills Builder Workbook

9

CAMBRIDGE
UNIVERSITY PRESS

CAMBRIDGE
UNIVERSITY PRESS

University Printing House, Cambridge CB2 8BS, United Kingdom

One Liberty Plaza, 20th Floor, New York, NY 10006, USA

477 Williamstown Road, Port Melbourne, VIC 3207, Australia

314–321, 3rd Floor, Plot 3, Splendor Forum, Jasola District Centre, New Delhi – 110025, India

103 Penang Road, #05-06/07, Visioncrest Commercial, Singapore 238467

Cambridge University Press is part of the University of Cambridge.

It furthers the University's mission by disseminating knowledge in the pursuit of education, learning and research at the highest international levels of excellence.

www.cambridge.org
Information on this title: www.cambridge.org/9781316637401 (Paperback)

First published 2017

20 19 18 17 16 15 14 13 12 11 10 9 8

Produced for Cambridge University Press by
White-Thomson Publishing
www.wtpub.co.uk

Editor: Sonya Newland
Designer: Ann Dixon
Illustrator: Ron Dixon

Printed in Great Britain by CPI Group (UK) Ltd, Croydon CR0 4YY

A catalogue record for this publication is available from the British Library

ISBN 978-1-316-63740-1 Paperback

Contents

Introduction

Welcome to Cambridge Checkpoint Mathematics Skills Builder Workbook 9.

The *Cambridge Checkpoint Mathematics* course covers the Cambridge Secondary 1 Mathematics curriculum framework. The course is divided into three stages: 7, 8 and 9.

You can use this Skills Builder Workbook with Coursebook 9 and Practice Book 9. It gives you extra practice in all the topics, focusing on those that are the most important, to improve your understanding and confidence.

Like the Coursebook and the Practice Book, this Workbook is divided into 19 units. In each unit there are exercises on each topic. There are introductory explanations and either worked examples or guided questions. These explain the skills you need to master and use to solve more complex problems. This Workbook also gives you a chance to try further questions on your own. This will improve your understanding of the units. It will also help you feel confident about working on your own when there is no teacher to help you. At the end of each unit is a link to exercises to attempt in the Coursebook.

If you get stuck with a task:

- Read the question again.
- Look back at the introductory explanations and worked examples or guided questions.
- Read through the matching section in the Coursebook.

1 Integers, powers and roots

1.1 Directed numbers

To subtract a negative number, you add the inverse. Look at these examples:

3 – –2 = 3 + 2 = 5   –2 – –5 = –2 + 5 = 3   –6 – –4 = –6 + 4 = –2

1 Fill in the missing numbers.

a 5 – –1 = 5 + ... = ...

b 2 – –4 = 2 + ... = ...

c 8 – –1 = 8 + ... = ...

d –3 – –1 = –3 + ... = ...

e –1 – –5 = –1 + ... = ...

f –7 – –5 = –7 + ... = ...

The numbers can be decimals:

2.5 – –1.3 = 2.5 + 1.3 = 3.8   –1.2 – –3.4 = –1.2 + 3.4 = 2.2

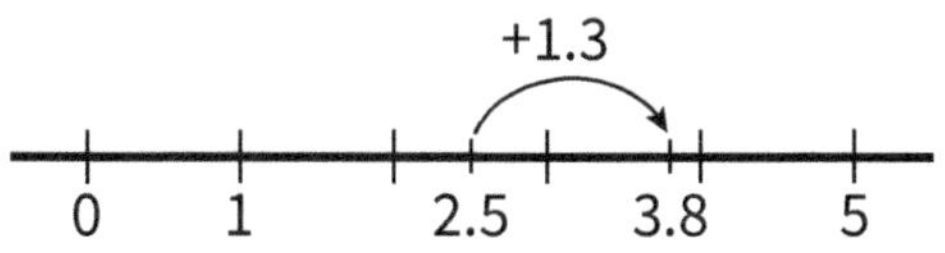

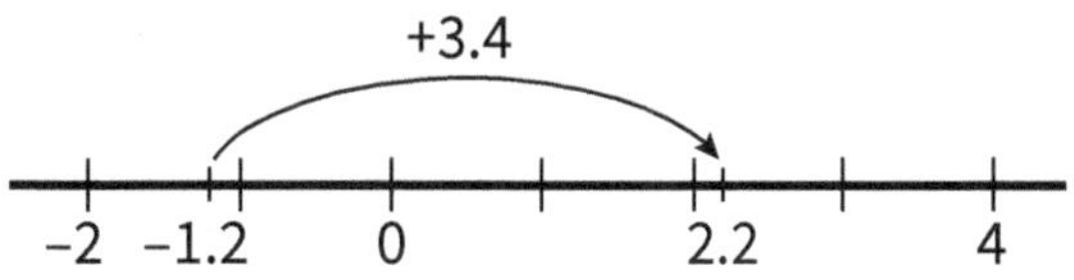

2 Fill in the missing numbers.

a 3.5 – –1.2 = 3.5 + ... = ...

b 2.2 – –3.4 = 2.2 + ... = ...

c 2.7 – –2.2 = 2.7 + ... = ...

d –4.6 – –2 = –4.6 + ... = ...

e –2 – –3.5 = –2 + ... = ...

f –6 – –2.3 = –6 + ... = ...

3 Fill in the missing outputs.

Input	Subtract	Output
–4 →		→ –1.5
2.5 →		→ ......
3.1 →	– –2.5	→ ......
–1.6 →		→ ......
–5.5 →		→ ......

The rule for multiplication is:

Same signs	3 × 4 = 12	positive answer
	–2 × –7 = 14	
Different signs	3 × –4 = –12	negative answer
	–2 × 7 = –14	

4 Complete these multiplications.

a 3 × –4 = ...

b –2 × –3 = ...

c –5 × 4 = ...

d 2.4 × –2 = ...

e –3.2 × 3 = ...

f –4.1 × –5 = ...

5 Fill in the missing outputs.

Input	Multiply	Output
3 →		→ –9
–4.2 →		→ ......
2.5 →	× –3	→ ......
–1.2 →		→ ......
–6.1 →		→ ......

Now try Exercise 1.1 on page 8 of Coursebook 9.

1.2 Square roots and cube roots

This number line shows the squares of whole numbers from 1 to 7.

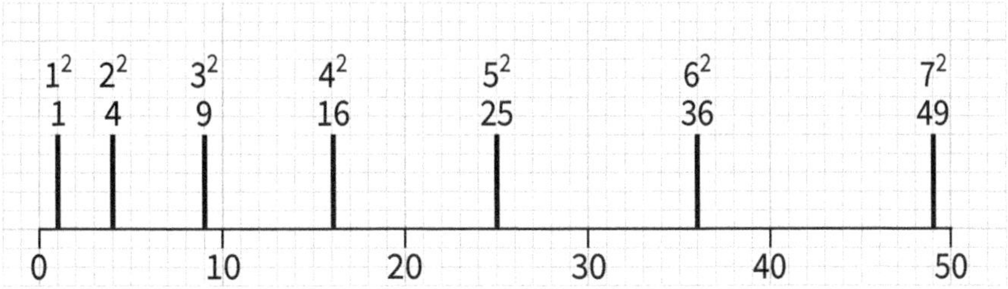

The square of 3 is 9 $3^2 = 9$ The square root of 9 is 3 $\sqrt{9} = 3$

1 Fill in the missing numbers.

a The square of 6 is ...... $6^2 =$ ...... The square root of ...... is 6 $\sqrt{......} = 6$

b The square of ...... is 25 $......^2 = 25$ The square root of 25 is ...... $\sqrt{25} =$ ......

2 Fill in the missing numbers.

a $\sqrt{49} =$ ...... **b** $\sqrt{4} =$ ...... **c** $\sqrt{16} =$ ...... **d** $\sqrt{1} =$ ......

What is $\sqrt{30}$? Look at the number line above.

30 is between 25 and 36.

So $\sqrt{30}$ is between 5 and 6.

25 is 5^2 and 36 is 6^2.

3 Fill in the missing numbers.

a $\sqrt{20}$ is between ...... and ......

b $\sqrt{45}$ is between ...... and ......

c $\sqrt{14}$ is between ...... and ......

d $\sqrt{6}$ is between ...... and ......

e $\sqrt{27}$ is between ...... and ......

f $\sqrt{39}$ is between ...... and ......

4 Mark 7^2, 8^2, 9^2 and 10^2 on this number line.

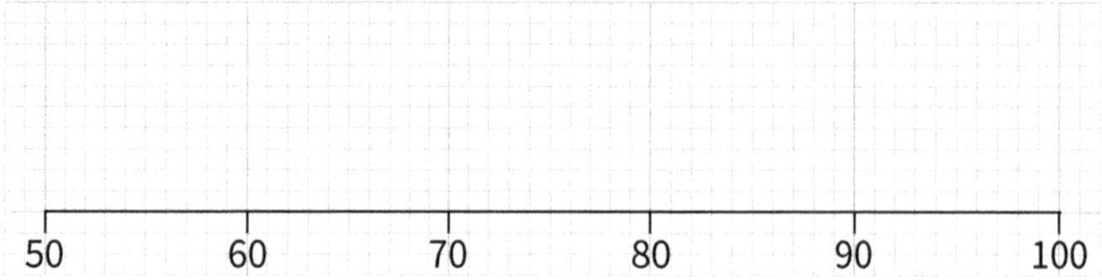

5 Mark 10^2, 11^2 and 12^2 on this number line.

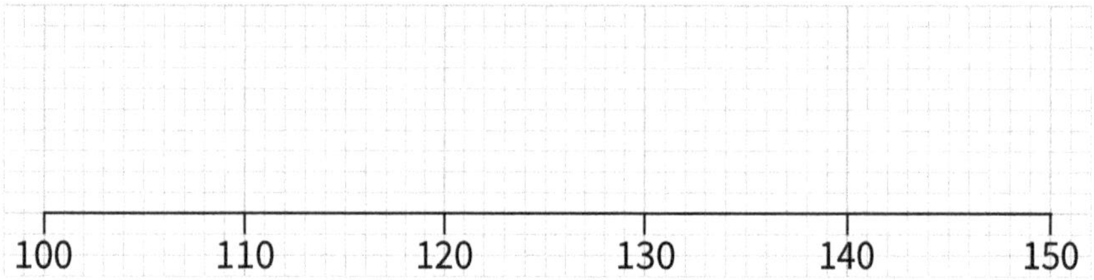

6 Fill in the missing numbers.

a $\sqrt{60}$ is between ...... and ......

b $\sqrt{93}$ is between ...... and ......

c $\sqrt{129}$ is between ...... and ......

d $\sqrt{108}$ is between ...... and ......

e $\sqrt{52}$ is between ...... and ......

f $\sqrt{77}$ is between ...... and ......

This number line shows the first five cube numbers.

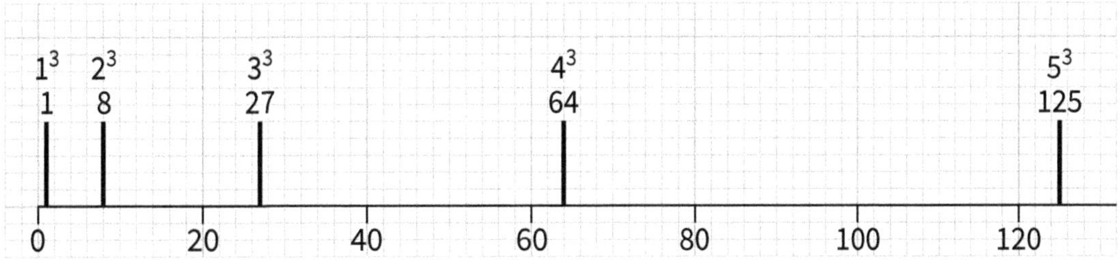

The cube of 4 is 64 $4^3 = 64$

$4^3 = 4 \times 4 \times 4$.

The cube root of 64 is 4 $\sqrt[3]{64} = 4$

7 Fill in the missing numbers.

a $\sqrt[3]{27} =$ ......

b $\sqrt[3]{8} =$ ......

c $\sqrt[3]{125} =$ ......

d $\sqrt[3]{1} =$ ......

8 Fill in the missing numbers.

a $\sqrt[3]{40}$ is between ...... and ......

b $\sqrt[3]{85}$ is between ...... and ......

c $\sqrt[3]{121}$ is between ...... and ......

d $\sqrt[3]{20}$ is between ...... and ......

e $\sqrt[3]{5}$ is between ...... and ......

f $\sqrt[3]{100}$ is between ...... and ......

Now try Exercise 1.2 on page 10 of Coursebook 9.

1.3 Indices

3^{-1} is another way of writing the fraction $\frac{1}{3}$

7^{-1} is another way of writing the fraction $\frac{1}{7}$

When you write 3^{-1}, the −1 is called an **index**. The plural is **indices**.

1 Write these numbers as fractions.

a 2^{-1} ......

b 6^{-1} ......

c 8^{-1} ......

d 10^{-1} ......

2 Write these fractions using indices.

a $\frac{1}{5}$ = ...

b $\frac{1}{12}$ = ...

c $\frac{1}{9}$ = ...

d $\frac{1}{4}$ = ...

$5^2 = 25$

You can write $\frac{1}{25} = 5^{-2}$

3 Fill in the missing numbers. The first one has been done for you.

a $4^2 = 16$ so $\frac{1}{16} = 4^{-2}$

b $6^2 = 36$ so $\frac{1}{36}$ = ...

c $10^2 = 100$ so ......

d $9^2 = 81$ so ......

e $7^2 = 49$ so ......

f $8^2 = 64$ so ......

Now try Exercise 1.3 on page 11 of Coursebook 9.

2 Sequences and functions

2.1 Generating sequences

This sequence of numbers is called a **linear** sequence: 2, 5, 8, 11, 14, …

In a linear sequence, the terms increase or decrease by the same amount each time.

The **term-to-term rule** for this sequence is 'Add 3'.

2 + 3 = 5, 5 + 3 = 8, 8 + 3 = 11, etc.

1 Write down the first five terms of each linear sequence. Some of them have been started for you.

a 1st term: 5

term-to-term rule: 'Add 2'.

5 (+2) 7 (+2) 9 (+2) …… (+2) ……

b 1st term: 0

term-to-term rule: 'Add 3'.

0 (+3) 3 (+3) …… (+3) …… (+3) ……

c 1st term: 11

term-to-term rule: 'Subtract 2'.

11 (−2) …… (−2) …… (−2) …… (−2) ……

d 1st term: 210

term-to-term rule: 'Subtract 20'.

210 …… …… …… ……

e 1st term: 2

term-to-term rule: 'Add 0.5'.

2 (+0.5) …… (+0.5) …… (+0.5) …… (+0.5) …… (+0.5) ……

This sequence of numbers is called a **non-linear** sequence: 2, 5, 9, 14, 20, ...

In a non-linear sequence, the terms increase or decrease by a different amount each time.

The term-to-term rule for this sequence is

'Add 3, add 4, add 5, add 6, ...'.

$2 + 3 = 5, 5 + 4 = 9, 9 + 5 = 14, \ldots$

2 Write down the first five terms of each non-linear sequence. Some of them have been started for you.

a 1st term: 4

term-to-term rule: 'Add 1, add 2, add 3, ...'.

4 (+1) 5 (+2) 7 (+3) ...... (+4) ......

b 1st term: 5

term-to-term rule: 'Add 2, add 4, add 6, ...'.

5 (+2) 7 (+4) ...... (+6) ...... (+8) ......

c 1st term: 20

term-to-term rule: 'Subtract 3, subtract 4, subtract 5, ...'.

20 (−3) ...... (−4) ...... (−5) ...... (−6) ......

3 Look at these sequences. Two of them are linear and two are non-linear.

Write 'Linear' or 'Non-linear' next to each one.

a 0, 3, 8, 15, 24 ....

b 18, 20, 22, 24, 26 ....

c 30, 25, 20, 15, 10 ....

d 50, 49, 47, 44, 40 ....

Now try Exercise 2.1 on page 16 of Coursebook 9.

2.2 Finding the nth term

A linear sequence is also called an **arithmetic sequence**.

You can write the position-to-term rule of an arithmetic sequence as an expression called the **nth term**.

Look at this sequence: 2, 4, 6, 8, 10, ...

The position-to-term rule is: term = 2 × position number

The nth term expression is: $2n$ (which means $2 \times n$)

You can see that 'position number' and n are the same thing.

1st term: 2 × 1 = 2
2nd term: 2 × 2 = 4
3rd term: 2 × 3 = 6

position number n

1 The nth term of a sequence is $5n$. Complete the workings to find the first four terms of the sequence. The first one has been done for you.

1st term: $5 \times n = 5 \times 1 = 5$ 2nd term: $5 \times n = 5 \times 2 =$ ......

3rd term: $5 \times n = 5 \times 3 =$ ...... 4th term: $5 \times n = 5 \times$ ...... = ...

2 The nth term of a sequence is $8n$. Work out the first four terms of the sequence.

1st term: ....

2nd term: ....

3rd term: ....

4th term: ....

3 The nth term of a sequence is $n + 3$. Complete the workings to find the first four terms of the sequence.

1st term: $n + 3 = 1 + 3 = 4$ 2nd term: $n + 3 = 2 + 3 =$ ......

3rd term: $n + 3 =$ ...... $+ 3 =$ ...... 4th term: $n + 3 =$ ...... $+ 3 =$ ......

4 The nth term of a sequence is $n + 10$. Work out the first four terms of the sequence.

1st term: ....

2nd term: ....

3rd term: ....

4th term: ....

5 Complete the workings to find the 10th term of each of these sequences.

a nth term = $3n$ 10th term = 3×10 = ...

b nth term = $8n$ 10th term = $8 \times$ ...... = ...

c nth term = $n + 4$ 10th term = ... + ... = ...

d nth term = $n + 9$ 10th term = ... + ... = ...

In each of the nth term expressions, swap n for 10.

6 Draw a line connecting each nth term expression with the correct value for the 10th term. The first one has been done for you.

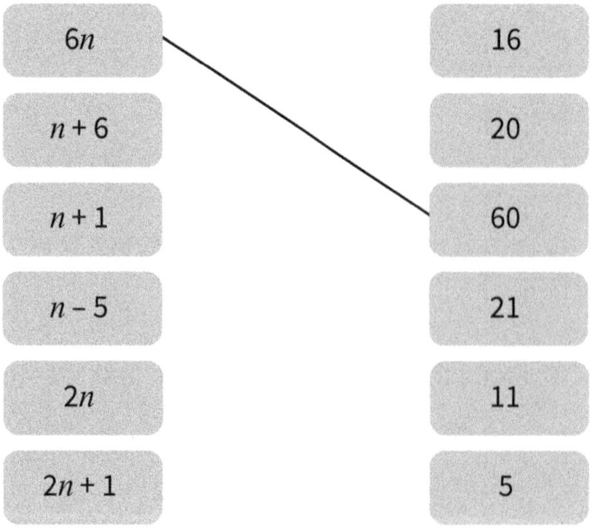

Now try Exercise 2.2 on page 19 of Coursebook 9.

2.3 Finding the inverse of a function

Here is a **function machine**.

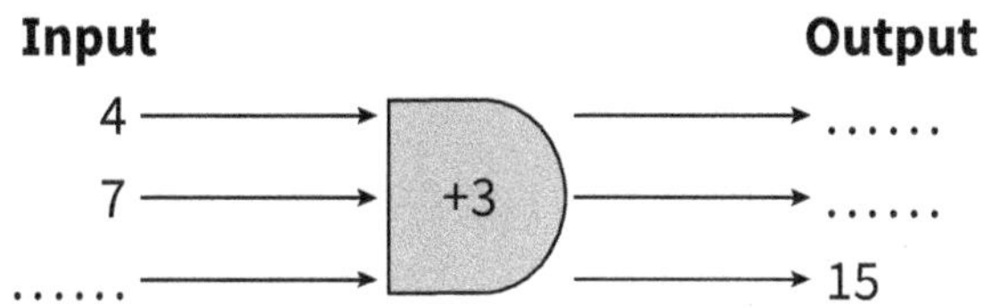

To work out the output values:

$4 + 3 = 7$
$7 + 3 = 10$

To work out the input value, reverse the function machine:

$15 - 3 = 12$

When you reverse the function machine you find the **inverse function**.

You can write a function and its inverse as a function machine like this:

Function:

Inverse:

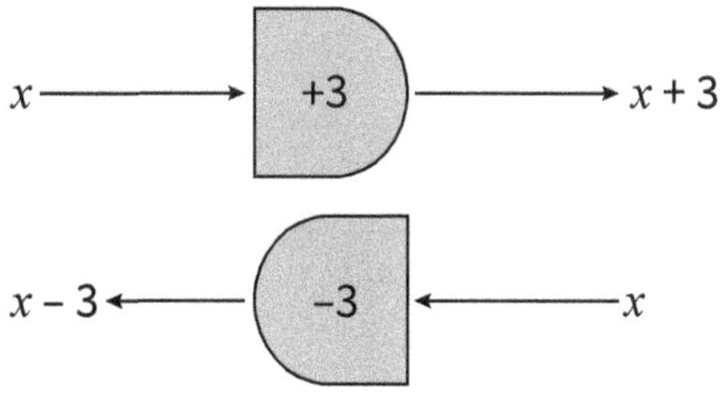

You can also write the function and its inverse as an equation:

Function: $y = x + 3$ Inverse: $y = x - 3$

Or you can write it as a mapping:

Function: $y \to x + 3$ Inverse: $y \to x - 3$

1 Work out the missing input and output numbers from these function machines.

a

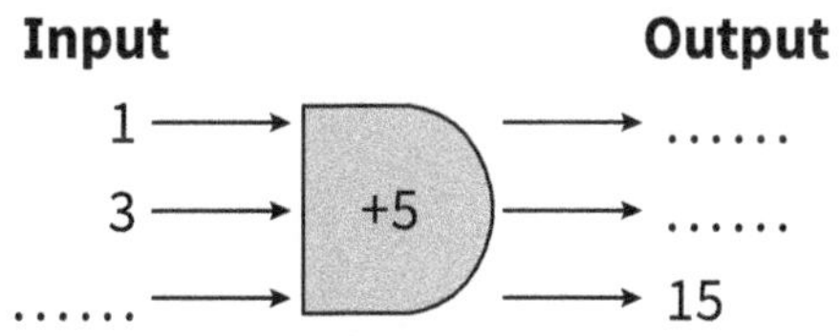

b

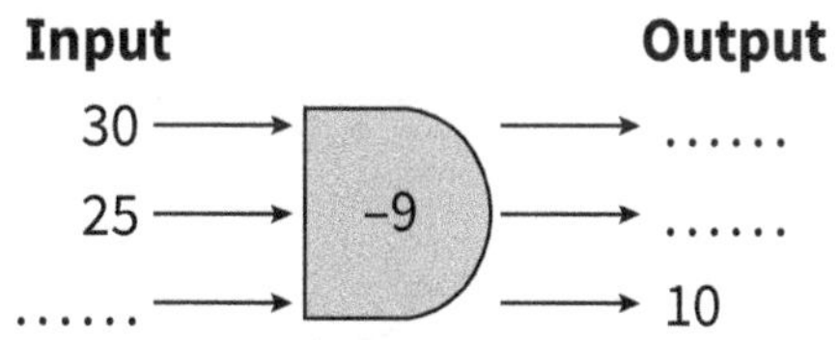

c

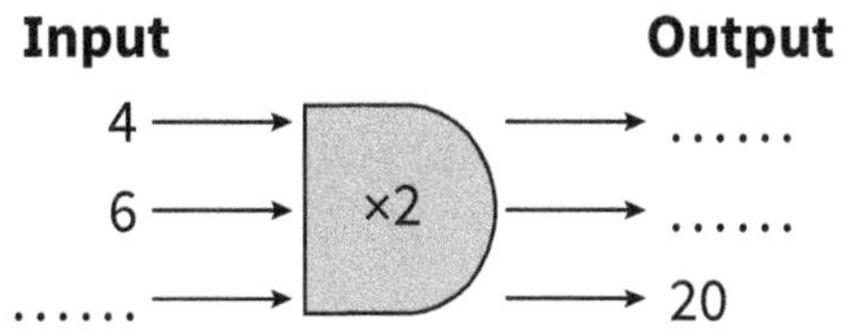

d

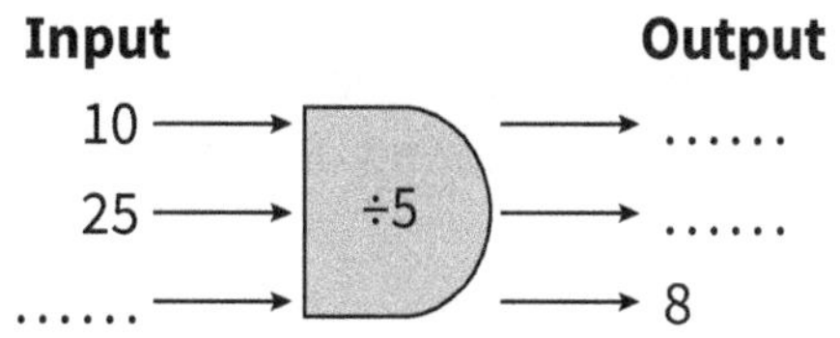

2 Complete the workings to find the inverse of each of these functions.
Use your answers to Question 1 to help you.

a 1 → [+5] → ...... x → [+5] → $x + 5$

1 ← [−5] ← 6 x − ...... ← [−5] ← x

b 30 → [−9] → ...... x → [−9] → $x - 9$

...... ← [+9] ← 21 x + ... ← [+9] ← x

c 4 → [×2] → ...... x → [×2] → $2x$

...... ← [÷2] ← 8 $\frac{x}{......}$ ← [÷2] ← x

d 10 → [÷2] → ...... x → [÷2] → $\frac{x}{2}$

...... ← [×2] ← 5 ...... x ← [×2] ← $\frac{x}{2}$

3 Find the inverse for each of these functions. Write each one as a machine, an equation and as a mapping. The first one has been done for you.

a

	Machine	Equation	Mapping
Function	x → [+4] → $x + 4$	$y = x + 4$	$x \rightarrow x + 4$
Inverse	$x - 4$ ← [−4] ← x	$y = x - 4$	$x \rightarrow x - 4$

b

Machine			Equation	Mapping
Function	x → [+7] →	$x + 7$	$y =$	$x \rightarrow$..........
Inverse	...... ← [......] ←	x	$y =$	$x \rightarrow$..........

c

Machine			Equation	Mapping
Function	x → [−6] →	$x - 6$	....	....
Inverse	...... ← [......] ←	x	....	....

d

Machine			Equation	Mapping
Function	x → [×9] →	$9x$	....	....
Inverse	...... ← [......] ←	x	....	....

e

Machine			Equation	Mapping
Function	x → [÷4] →	$\frac{x}{4}$	....	....
Inverse	...... ← [......] ←	x	....	....

Now try Exercise 2.3 on page 20 of Coursebook 9.

3 Place value, ordering and rounding

3.1 Multiplying and dividing decimals mentally

When you multiply and divide by decimals mentally, you can use **jottings** to help you.

Here is an example of how you can work out 8×0.3:

$8 \times 3 = 24$

$8 \times 0.3 = 2.4$

This method works because you change the 0.3 to 3 by multiplying by 10: $0.3 \times \mathbf{10} = 3$

Then you divide the answer of 24 by 10: $24 \div \mathbf{10} = 2.4$

1 Fill in the missing numbers to work out these mental multiplications.

a	4×0.3	$4 \times 3 = 12$	so	$4 \times 0.3 =$ ......
b	7×0.4	$7 \times 4 =$	so	$7 \times 0.4 =$ ......
c	9×0.1	$9 \times 1 =$	so	$9 \times 0.1 =$ ......
d	15×0.2	$15 \times 2 =$	so	$15 \times 0.2 =$ ......
e	8×0.02	$8 \times 2 = 16$	so	$8 \times 0.02 =$ ......
f	5×0.04	$5 \times 4 =$	so	$5 \times 0.04 =$ ......
g	11×0.07	$11 \times 7 =$	so	$11 \times 0.07 =$ ......

Here is an example of a method you can use to work out 12 ÷ 0.3:

12 × 10 = 120
0.3 × 10 = 3
120 ÷ 3 = 40

You multiply both numbers by 10 so that the 0.3 becomes a whole number instead of a decimal.

This method works because when you are dividing two numbers, if you multiply both numbers by 10, 100 or any other number, the answer to the division will remain the same.

2 Fill in the missing numbers to work out these mental divisions.

a	6 ÷ 0.3	6 × 10 = 60	0.3 × 10 = 3	60 ÷ 3 = ...
b	8 ÷ 0.2	8 × 10 = 80	0.2 × 10 = ...	80 ÷ ...... = ...
c	9 ÷ 0.1	9 × 10 = ...	0.1 × 10 = ...	...... ÷ ...... = ...
d	12 ÷ 0.4	12 × 10 = ...	0.4 × 10 = ...	...... ÷ ...... = ...
e	6 ÷ 0.02	6 × 100 = 600	0.02 × 100 = 2	600 ÷ 2 = ...
f	8 ÷ 0.04	8 × 100 = ...	0.04 × 100 = ...	...... ÷ ...... = ...
g	16 ÷ 0.08	16 × 100 = ...	0.08 × 100 = ...	...... ÷ ...... = ...

Now try Exercise 3.1 on page 24 of Coursebook 9.

3.2 Multiplying and dividing by powers of 10

When you multiply and divide numbers by powers of 10, it is easiest to start by changing the power of 10 into a normal number.

For example, $\times 10^3$ means $\times 1000$, because 10^3 means $10 \times 10 \times 10 = 1000$.

1 Draw a line from each rectangular card to its matching oval card. One has been done for you.

Rectangular cards	Oval cards
$\times 10^0$	×1000
$\times 10^1$	×1
$\times 10^2$	×10 000
$\times 10^3$	×100
$\times 10^4$	×100 000
$\times 10^5$	×10

When you multiply, use this method of moving the decimal point:

$5.8 \times 10^2 = 5.8 \times 100 = 580$

Move the decimal point two places to the right as 100 has two zeros. 5.8.0.

2 Complete the workings for each of these multiplications.

a $3.4 \times 10^2 = 3.4 \times$ ...... = ...

b $4.8 \times 10^3 = 4.8 \times$ ...... = ...

c $12.5 \times 10^1 = 12.5 \times$ ...... = ...

d $5 \times 10^5 = 5 \times$ ...... = ...

e $14 \times 10^3 = 14 \times$ ...... = ...

After you have moved the decimal point, remember to fill in any spaces in the answers with zeros.

Hint: 5 = 5.0

3 Draw a line from each rectangular card to its matching oval card.

$\times 10^{-1}$	$\div 10\,000$
$\times 10^{-2}$	$\div 10$
$\times 10^{-3}$	$\div 100\,000$
$\times 10^{-4}$	$\div 1000$
$\times 10^{-5}$	$\div 100$

When you divide, use this method of moving the decimal point:

$5.8 \times 10^{-2} = 5.8 \div 100 = 0.058$

> Move the decimal point two places to the left as 100 has two zeros.
>
> 0.0.5.8

4 Complete the workings for each of these divisions.

a $3.4 \times 10^{-2} = 3.4 \div$ ...... = ...

b $8 \times 10^{-3} = 8 \div$ ...... = ...

c $15 \times 10^{-4} = 15 \div$ ...... = ...

d $12 \times 10^{-1} = 12 \div$ ...... = ...

> After you have moved the decimal point, remember to fill in any spaces in the answers with zeros.

Now try Exercise 3.2 on page 27 of Coursebook 9.

3.3 Rounding

Use this method to round a decimal number to one decimal place (1 d.p.).

Round 5.623 to 1 d.p.

Underline the digit in first place after the point: 5 . 6 2 3

Circle the next digit: 5 . 6 (2) 3

The number in the circle is **less than 5**, so leave the underlined number as it is: 5 . 6

Round 5.693 to 1 d.p.

Underline the digit in first place after the point: 5 . 6 9 3

Circle the next digit: 5 . 6 (9) 3

The number in the circle is **5 or more**, so add 1 to the underlined number: 5 . 7

1 Round each of these numbers to 1 d.p.

a 4.12 ......

b 3.85 ......

c 6.337 ......

d 8.164 ......

e 12.77 ......

f 43.05 ......

2 Round each of these numbers to 2 d.p.

a 5.168 ......

b 5.223 ......

c 0.7769 ......

d 0.0444 ......

e 12.005 ......

f 25.118 ......

This time, underline the second digit and put a circle round the third, then follow the same method as above.

3 All the following numbers have been rounded to 3 d.p.

Put a tick (✓) if they are correct and a cross (✗) if they are wrong.

If they are wrong, write the correct rounded answer.

a 5.6647 correct to 3 d.p. is 5.665 ......

b 3.1212 correct to 3 d.p. is 3.121 ......

c 0.0079 correct to 3 d.p. is 0.08 ......

d 12.0454 correct to 3 d.p. is 12.045 ......

Now try Exercise 3.3 on page 29 of Coursebook 9.

3.4 Order of operations

When you carry out calculations, you must use the correct **order of operations**.

B	**I**	**D**	**M**	**A**	**S**
Brackets	**I**ndices (powers)	**D**ivision	**M**ultiplication	**A**ddition	**S**ubtraction

Write down the operations you have to do for each calculation, then do them in the right order. For example:

$5 + 3 \times 6$

$5 + 3 \times 6$
(+ is A, × is M)
$= 5 + 18$
$= 23$

M comes before A in the list, so Multiply and then Add
M: 3 x 6 = 18
A: 5 + 18 = 23

1 Complete the table showing the workings for each of these calculations.

The first one has been done for you.

	Calculation	Operations	Order of operations	1st step	2nd step
a	$20 - 4 \times 3$	S and M	M then S	$4 \times 3 = 12$	$20 - 12 = 8$
b	$8 \times 2 + 4$	M and A	M then A		
c	$3 + \frac{8}{2}$	A and D			
d	$\frac{30}{6} - 1$	D and S			
e	$7 + 2^2$	A and I			
f	$2 \times (9 + 11)$	M and B			
g	$50 - (30 - 10)$	S and B			
h	$5^2 - 15$	I and S			

2 Complete the workings for these calculations.

a $3 \times 2 + 4 \times 2$ Ms then A $3 \times 2 = 6$ $4 \times 2 = \ldots\ldots$ $6 + \ldots\ldots = \ldots\ldots$

M A M

b $2^2 + 5 \times 3$ I then M then A $2^2 = \ldots\ldots$ $5 \times 3 = \ldots\ldots$ $\ldots\ldots + \ldots\ldots = \ldots\ldots$

I A M

c $\frac{20}{2} - 3^2$ I then D then S $3^2 = \ldots\ldots$ $20 \div 2 = \ldots\ldots$ $\ldots\ldots - \ldots\ldots = \ldots\ldots$

D S I

Now try Exercise 3.4 on page 30 of Coursebook 9.

4 Length, mass, capacity and time

4.1 Solving problems involving measurements

When you solve problems involving measurements, you need to be able to convert metric units.

1 Complete these conversion tables.

Length
1 km = ... m
1 m = ... cm
1 cm = ... mm

Mass
1 kg = ... g

Capacity
1 l = ... ml

2 Complete these conversions of length. Use the flow charts to help you.

km → × 1000 → m → × 100 → cm → × 10 → mm

a 5 km = ... m

b 4.5 m = ... cm

c 3.2 cm = ... mm

d 0.25 km = ... m

km ← ÷ 1000 ← m ← ÷ 100 ← cm ← ÷ 10 ← mm

e 700 cm = ... m

f 450 mm = ... cm

g 3200 m = ... km

h 1250 cm = ... m

3 Complete these conversions of mass. Use the flow charts to help you.

kg → × 1000 → g

kg ← ÷ 1000 ← g

a) 5 kg = ... g

b) 3.2 kg = ... g

c) 0.5 kg = ... g

d) 2600 g = ... kg

e) 250 g = ... kg

f) 14 000 g = ... kg

4 Complete these conversions of capacity. Use the flow charts to help you.

l → × 1000 → ml

l ← ÷ 1000 ← ml

a) 8 l = ... ml

b) 12 l = ... ml

c) 2.4 l = ... ml

d) 9000 ml = ... l

e) 3500 ml = ... l

f) 750 ml = ... l

Now try Exercise 4.1 on page 35 of Coursebook 9.

4.2 Solving problems involving average speed

When you solve problems involving **average speed** you must be able to convert between fraction and decimal hours of time.

1 Draw lines linking the minutes to their equivalent fraction and decimal of an hour.

Minutes
15
30
45

Fraction of an hour
$\frac{1}{2}$
$\frac{3}{4}$
$\frac{1}{4}$

Decimal of an hour
0.75
0.25
0.5

2 Convert each fraction of an hour into minutes.

a $\frac{1}{3}$ = 60 ÷ 3 = ... minutes

b $\frac{1}{5}$ = 60 ÷ ...... = ... minutes

c $\frac{1}{6}$ = 60 ÷ ...... = ... minutes

d $\frac{1}{10}$ = 60 ÷ ...... = ... minutes

e $\frac{2}{3}$ = 60 ÷ 3 = ... × 2 = ... minutes

f $\frac{4}{5}$ = 60 ÷ 5 = ... × ...... = ... minutes

3 Convert each number of minutes into a fraction of an hour.

a 6 mins = $\frac{6}{60}$ = $\frac{1}{\square}$ hour

b 4 mins = $\frac{\square}{60}$ = $\frac{1}{\square}$ hour

c 24 mins = $\frac{\square}{60}$ = $\frac{\square}{\square}$ hour

d 50 mins = $\frac{\square}{60}$ = $\frac{\square}{\square}$ hour

Write the minutes as a fraction over 60, then simplify it by cancelling common factors.

4 Convert each decimal of an hour into minutes. The first one has been done for you.

> Always multiply the decimal of an hour by 60 to work out the number of minutes.

a 0.1 = 0.1 × 60 = 6 minutes

b 0.2 = 0.2 × 60 = ... minutes

c 0.6 = ... × 60 = ... minutes

d 0.9 = ... × 60 = ... minutes

You can calculate the average speed for a journey using this formula:

$$\text{speed} = \frac{\text{distance}}{\text{time}}$$

5 Complete the working to calculate the average speed for each of these journeys. The first one has been done for you.

> Write the formula first, then substitute the numbers into the formula.

a distance = 160 km time = 2 hours

$$\text{speed} = \frac{\text{distance}}{\text{time}} = \frac{160}{2} = 80 \text{ km/h}$$

> When the distance is in km and the time is in hours, the speed is in kilometres per hour (km/h).

b distance = 180 km time = 3 hours

$$\text{speed} = \frac{\text{distance}}{\text{time}} = \frac{\square}{\square} = \text{......} \text{ km/h}$$

c distance = 450 km time = 5 hours

$$\text{speed} = \frac{\text{distance}}{\text{time}} = \frac{\square}{\square} = \text{......} \text{ km/h}$$

6 Complete the working to calculate the average speed for each of these journeys.

Start by writing each time as a decimal number of hours.

a distance = 60 km time = $2\frac{1}{2}$ hours = ... hours

speed = $\frac{\text{distance}}{\text{time}} = \frac{\square}{\square}$ = ... km/h

Write $2\frac{1}{2}$ as a decimal number of hours here.

b distance = 286 km time = $3\frac{1}{4}$ hours = ... hours

speed = $\frac{\text{distance}}{\text{time}} = \frac{\square}{\square}$ = ... km/h

c distance = 112 km time = $1\frac{3}{4}$ hours = ... hours

speed = $\frac{\text{distance}}{\text{time}} = \frac{\square}{\square}$ = ... km/h

You calculate the distance of a journey using this formula: distance = speed × time

7 Complete the working to calculate the distance for each of these journeys.

a speed = 25 km/h time = 2 hours

distance = speed × time = 25 × 2 = ... km

b speed = 70 km/h time = 4 hours

distance = speed × time = ... × ...... = ... km

Now try Exercise 4.2 on page 36 of Coursebook 9.

4.3 Using compound measures

Compound measures are measures such as kilometres per hour, cents per gram and dollars per litre. They are made up of mixed units. You can use compound measures to compare speeds of journeys and costs of items.

Complete the workings in the questions below.

1 A small bag of 6 packets of crisps costs \$7.20.

A large bag of 10 packets of crisps costs \$13.

Which bag is the best value for money?

Small bag: cost per packet = \$7.20 ÷ 6 = \$......

Large bag: cost per packet = \$13 ÷ 10 = \$......

The .... bag is the best value for money because ....

....

2 A 200 ml bottle of water costs \$1.40.

A 500 ml bottle of water costs \$3.25.

Change the dollars into cents to make the calculations easier.

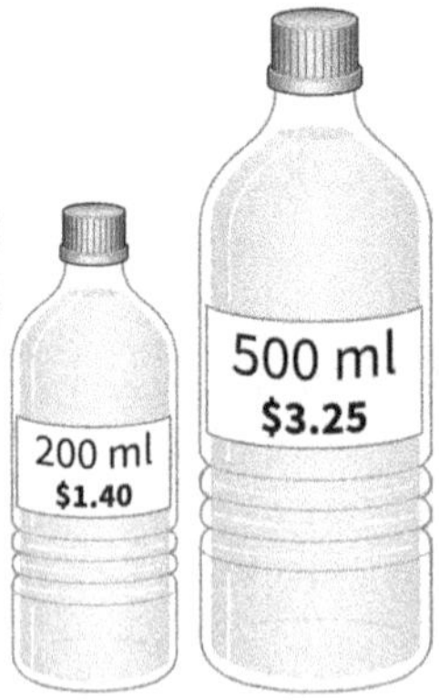

Which bottle is the best value for money?

Small bottle: cost per ml = 140 ÷ 200 = ... cents per ml

Large bottle: cost per ml = 325 ÷ 500 = ... cents per ml

The .... bottle is the best value for money because ....

....

3 A train takes 2 hours to travel 240 km.

A second train takes 3 hours to travel 345 km.

Which train is the quickest?

First train: speed = $\frac{\text{distance}}{\text{time}} = \frac{\square}{\square} =$ ...... km/h

Second train: speed = $\frac{\text{distance}}{\text{time}} = \frac{\square}{\square} =$ ...... km/h

The ...... train is the quickest.

To work out which train is the quickest, you need to work out the speed of each one using the formula

speed = $\frac{\text{distance}}{\text{time}}$

Now try Exercise 4.3 on page 38 of Coursebook 9.

5 Shapes

5.1 Regular polygons

A **polygon** is a shape with straight sides.
All the sides of a regular polygon are equal.
All the angles of a regular polygon are equal.

You can find the size of each angle of a regular polygon.

This regular polygon has three sides. It is an equilateral triangle.
Multiply 180 × (number of sides – 2).
180 × 1 = 180
Divide by the number of sides.
180 ÷ 3 = 60
Each angle is 60°.

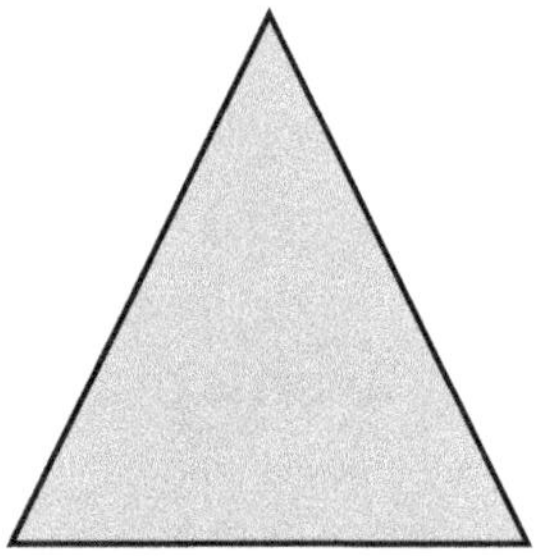

This regular polygon has four sides. It is a square.
Multiply 180 × (number of sides – 2).
180 × 2 = 360
Divide by the number of sides.
360 ÷ 4 = 90
Each angle is 90°.

1. Complete this calculation.

   This regular polygon has 5 sides. It is a ....

   Multiply 180 × (number of sides – 2): 180 × 3 = ...

   Divide by the number of sides: ...... ÷ 5 = ...

   Each angle is ......°

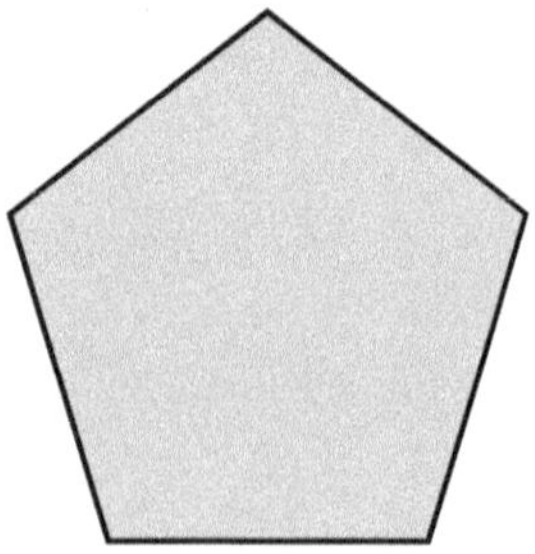

2. Complete this calculation.

   This regular polygon has ...... sides. It is a ....

   Multiply 180 × (number of sides – 2): 180 × ...... = ...

   Divide by the number of sides: ...... ÷ ...... = ...

   Each angle is ......°

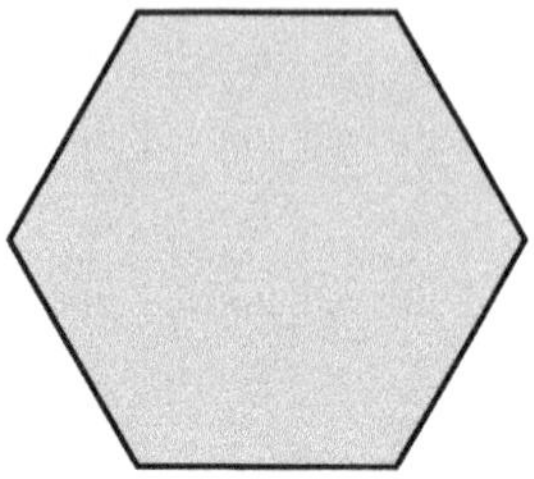

3 Complete this calculation.

This regular polygon has ...... sides. It is an octagon.

Multiply 180 × (number of sides – 2): 180 × ...... = ...

Divide by the number of sides: ...... ÷ ...... = ...

Each angle is ......°

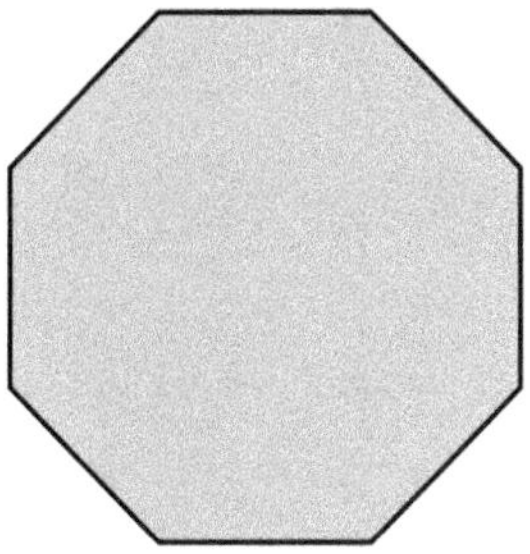

4 Complete this calculation.

This regular polygon has ...... sides. It is a decagon.

Multiply 180 × (number of sides – 2): 180 × ...... = ...

Divide by the number of sides: ...... ÷ ...... = ...

Each angle is ......°

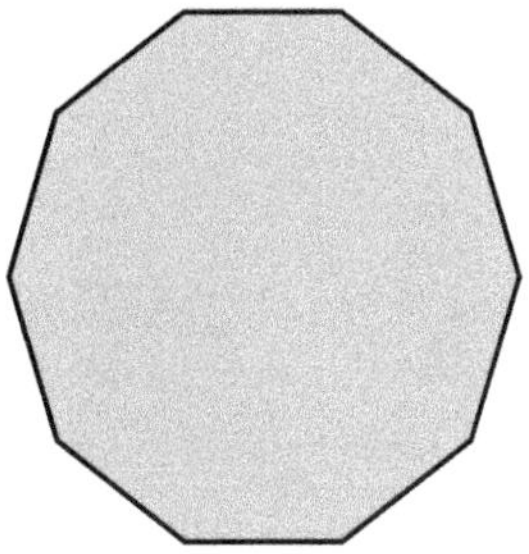

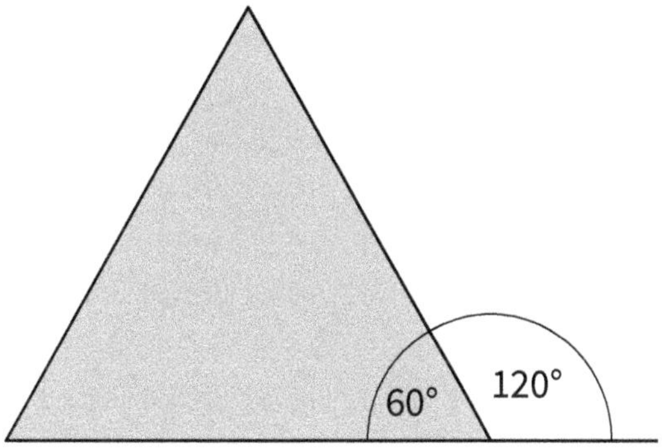

The angle inside this regular triangle is 60°. This is called the **interior angle**.

The other angle marked is the **exterior angle**.

The exterior angle = 180° – the interior angle = 180 – 60 = 120°.

5 Write the size of the interior angle and the exterior angle on each regular polygon.

a

b

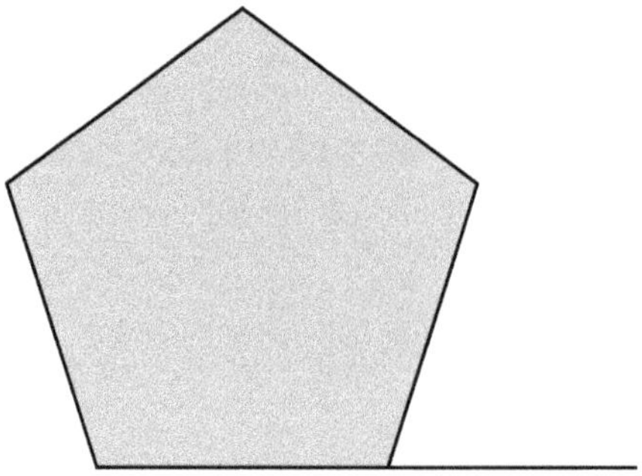

c

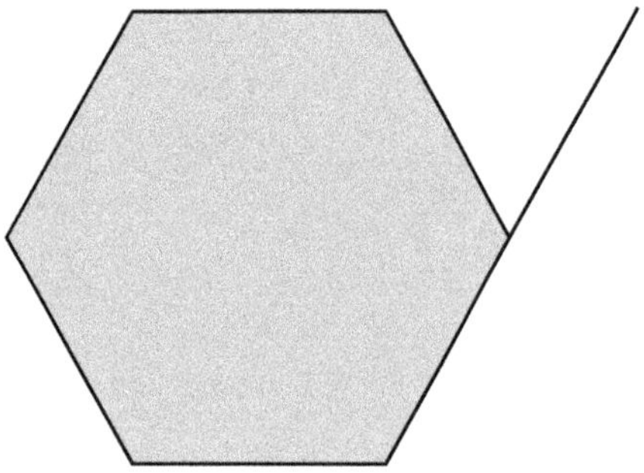

d

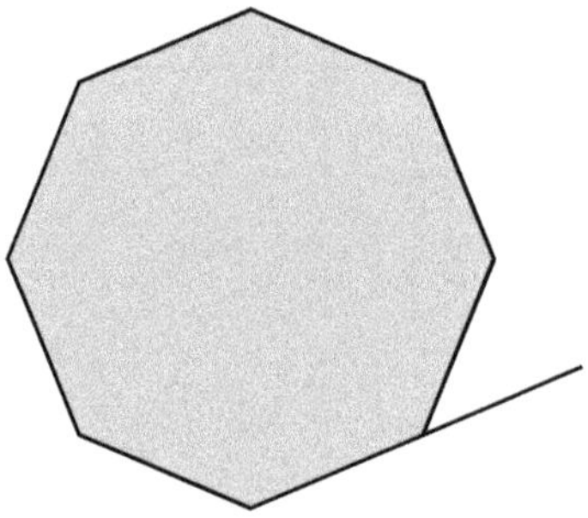

e

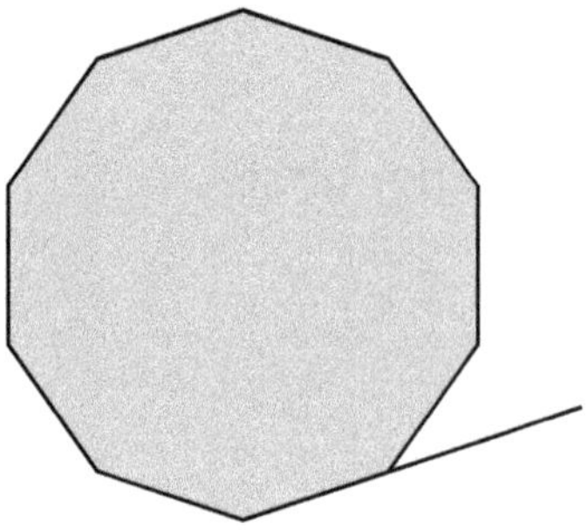

Now try Exercise 5.1 on page 42 of Coursebook 9.

5.2 Plans and elevations

Here are three cubes joined together.

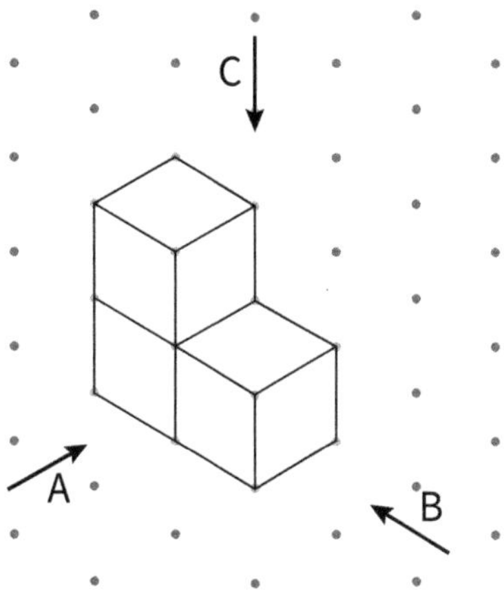

This is the view from arrow A.
You can see three cubes.

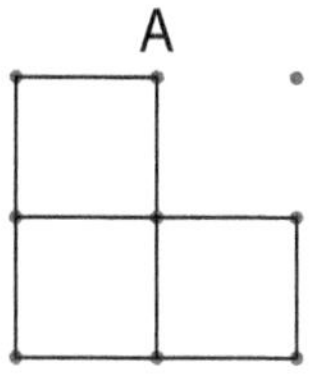

This is the view from arrow B
You can only see two cubes.

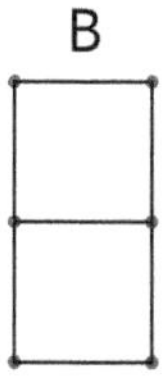

These are called **elevations**.

This is the overhead view from arrow C.

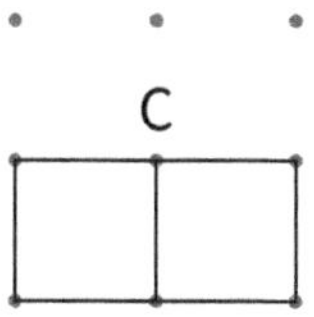

The overhead view is called a **plan**.

Each of the shapes below is made from cubes joined together.

Draw two elevations (A and B) and a plan (C) for each one.

1

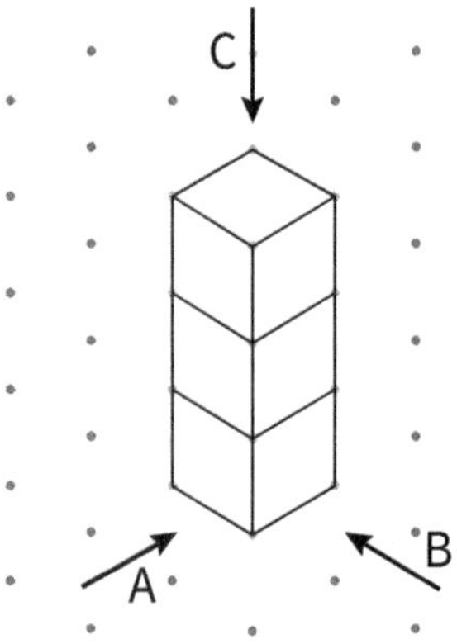

2

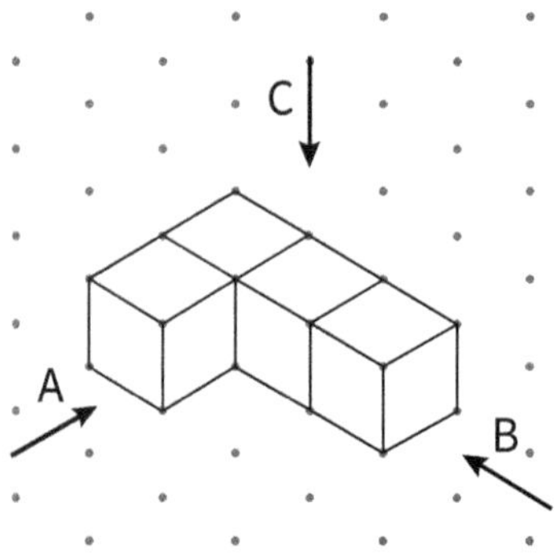

3

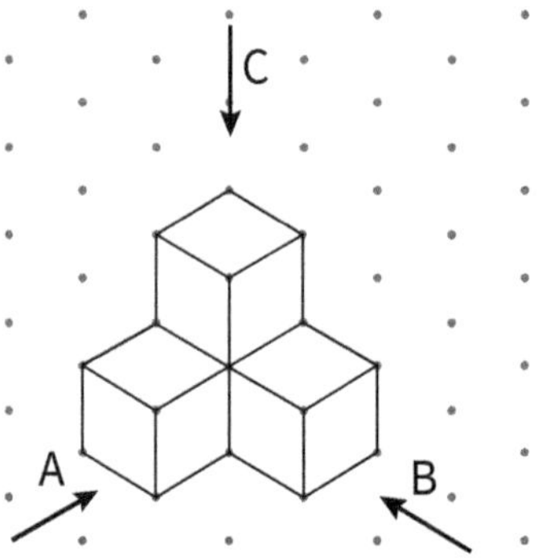

4

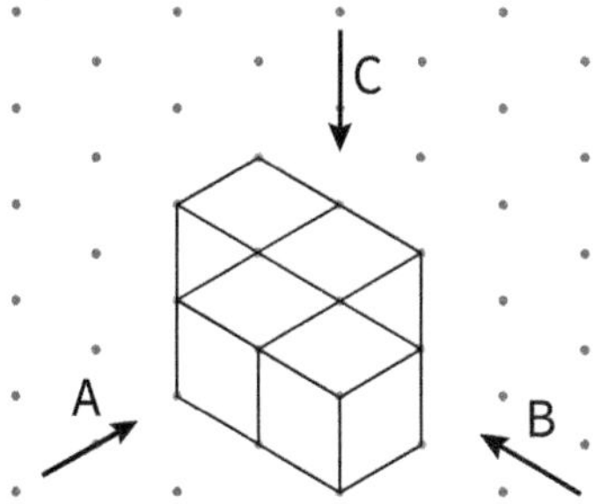

5

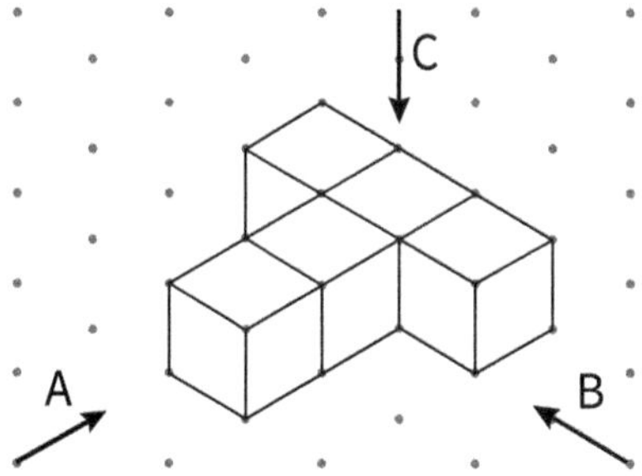

Now try Exercise 5.5 on page 51 of Coursebook 9.

6 Planning and collecting data

6.1 Designing data collection sheets

A **data collection sheet** is a frequency table that you fill in with information.

When completing a data collection sheet, you must make sure that:

- it includes all possible answers
- it is easy to quickly total all the tallies
- each answer only appears in one tally box
- there is a box for the total frequencies.

1 Hassan asks 40 students to choose their favourite Olympic sport out of athletics, gymnastics, cycling, swimming and badminton.

He designs four different frequency tables.

Here are the first three. Explain what is wrong with each one.

a

Sport	Tally	Frequency
Athletics		
Gymnastics		
Cycling		
Swimming		
	Total	

What is wrong: ....

....

b

Sport	Tally	Frequency
Athletics		
Gymnastics		
Rowing		
Swimming		
Badminton		
	Total	

What is wrong:

c

Sport	Tally	Frequency
Athletics		
Gymnastics		
Cycling		
Swimming		
Badminton		

What is wrong:

d When Hassan starts to fill in his tally chart, this is what he writes.

What has he done wrong so far?

Sport	Tally	Frequency
Athletics	ǀǀǀǀǀǀǀǀǀǀǀ	
Gymnastics	ǀǀǀǀǀǀǀǀǀǀǀǀǀǀǀǀ	
Cycling	ǀǀǀǀǀ	
Swimming	ǀǀǀǀǀǀǀǀ	
Badminton	ǀ	
	Total	

What is wrong:

2 Oditi rolls a dice 60 times and records the number she gets on each throw.

Finish the design of this data collection sheet for her.

Number on dice	**Tally**	
1		

The numbers on a dice go from 1 to 6.

3 Dakarai asks 50 students their favourite colour out of red, blue, green, yellow and orange.

Finish the design of this data collection sheet for him.

Colour		

Don't forget the 'Total' box.

4 Mia does a survey on the ages of people using a gym one day.

Here are the two data collection sheets she designs.

Design A

Age (years)	Tally	Frequency
0–20		
20–40		
40–60		
60+		
	Total	

Design B

Age (years)	Tally	Frequency
0–19		
20–39		
40–59		
60+		
	Total	

Which data collection sheet do you think is the best one for her to use?

Look at both designs to see where you would record an age of 20.

Explain your answer.

....

....

....

Now try Exercise 6.3 on page 60 of Coursebook 9.

6.2 Collecting data

When you collect data, you need to decide if your data collection sheet will record:

- individual names or values (e.g. the numbers on a dice 1, 2, 3, 4, 5, 6)
- grouped values (e.g. ages 0–19, 20–39, 40–59, 60+).

1 Xavier recorded the colour of the first 20 cars that drove past his school one morning. Here are his results:

~~Red~~	~~Silver~~	White	Black	Red	White	White	Black	Red	Red
Black	White	Red	Silver	Silver	White	Black	Black	Red	Red

a Complete this data-collection sheet.

Colour	Tally	Frequency
Red	I	
Black		
Silver	I	
White		
	Total	

Put a line through one colour at a time and record a tally in the table. Remember to use ~~IIII~~ for five tally marks. The first two have been done for you.

b Which is the most popular colour car? ....

c Make one other comment about what your data collection sheet tells you.

....

....

2 Tanesha has a four-sided dice. When she rolls the dice she gets one of the four numbers 1, 2, 3 or 4. Tanesha rolls the dice 25 times. Here are her results:

3	1	4	2	3	4	2	1	4	2	3	2	2
4	2	4	1	4	2	3	3	2	1	4	1	

a Complete this data collection sheet.

Number	Tally	Frequency
1		
2		
3		
4		
	Total	

b Which number was rolled most often? ....

c Make one other comment about what your data collection sheet tells you.

....

....

3 A cricket player records the number of runs she scores at each match for 20 matches. Here are her results:

22	75	98	55	45	84	15	70	32	57
42	51	29	31	62	58	105	57	88	21

a Complete this data collection sheet.

Number of runs	Tally	Frequency
0–29		
30–59		
60–89		
90–119		
	Total	

b Make one comment about what your data collection sheet tells you.

....

....

4 Razi records the mass, in grams, of 30 apples she picks from her tree.
Here are her results.

150	104	175	145	152	140	118	135	132	159
175	126	165	105	146	128	138	155	125	135
148	112	145	185	150	115	142	122	130	120

a Complete this data collection sheet.

This box shows that m represents mass in grams. → (points to the "Mass of apples, m (g)" heading)

This box shows that this row is for the apples which have a mass greater than 150 g, but less than or equal to 175 g. → (points to the $150 < m \leqslant 175$ row)

Mass of apples, m (g)	Tally	Frequency
$100 < m \leqslant 125$		
$125 < m \leqslant 150$		
$150 < m \leqslant 175$		
$175 < m \leqslant 200$		
	Total	

b Make one comment about what your data collection sheet tells you.

....

....

Now try Exercise 6.4 on page 61 of Coursebook 9.

7.1 Writing a fraction in its simplest form

When you write a fraction in its **simplest form**, you need to cancel common factors.

To help you do this, ask yourself these questions:

- Can I divide both numbers in the fraction by 2?
- Can I divide both numbers by 3?
- Can I divide both numbers by 5 or any other number?

1 Complete the workings to write each fraction in its simplest form.

a ÷2 ÷2: $\frac{8}{20} = \frac{4}{10} = \frac{\square}{\square}$ (÷2 ÷2)

b ÷2 ÷3: $\frac{6}{18} = \frac{\square}{\square} = \frac{\square}{\square}$ (÷2 ÷3)

c ÷2: $\frac{14}{22} = \frac{\square}{\square}$ (÷2)

d ÷2 ÷5: $\frac{30}{50} = \frac{\square}{\square} = \frac{\square}{\square}$ (÷2 ÷5)

e ÷2 ÷2 ÷2: $\frac{16}{24} = \frac{\square}{\square} = \frac{\square}{\square} = \frac{\square}{\square}$ (÷2 ÷2 ÷2)

f ÷7: $\frac{14}{21} = \frac{\square}{\square}$ (÷7)

2 The fractions in the rectangles have been written in their simplest forms in the ovals. Draw a line from each rectangle to the correct oval.

Show all your working below. All the divisions are shown in the cloud.

Rectangles	Ovals
$\frac{16}{20}$	$\frac{7}{10}$
$\frac{28}{40}$	$\frac{6}{7}$
$\frac{35}{45}$	$\frac{4}{5}$
$\frac{36}{42}$	$\frac{3}{4}$
$\frac{45}{60}$	$\frac{7}{9}$

÷5
÷2 and ÷2
÷3 and ÷5
÷2 and ÷3
÷2 and ÷2

Now try Exercise 7.1 on page 65 of Coursebook 9.

7.2 Adding and subtracting fractions

You can only add or subtract fractions when the denominators are the same.

1 Draw a line linking each calculation to its correct answer.
The first one has been done for you.

$\frac{1}{5}+\frac{3}{5}$	$\frac{3}{7}$
$\frac{5}{7}-\frac{2}{7}$	$\frac{3}{8}$
$\frac{2}{9}+\frac{5}{9}$	$\frac{3}{13}$
$\frac{5}{8}-\frac{2}{8}$	$\frac{5}{7}$
$\frac{3}{6}+\frac{2}{6}$	$\frac{4}{9}$
$\frac{9}{13}-\frac{6}{13}$	$\frac{4}{5}$
$\frac{6}{9}-\frac{2}{9}$	$\frac{7}{9}$
$\frac{4}{7}+\frac{1}{7}$	$\frac{5}{6}$

(Line drawn: $\frac{1}{5}+\frac{3}{5}$ → $\frac{4}{5}$)

2 Complete the workings for these additions and subtractions.

a $\frac{1}{3}+\frac{1}{9}=\frac{3}{9}+\frac{1}{9}=\frac{\square}{9}$

Change $\frac{1}{3}$ to $\frac{3}{9}$ like this $\frac{1\times 3}{3\times 3}=\frac{3}{9}$

b $\frac{11}{15}-\frac{1}{5}=\frac{11}{15}-\frac{\square}{15}=\frac{\square}{15}$

c $\frac{1}{6}+\frac{5}{12}=\frac{\square}{12}+\frac{5}{12}=\frac{\square}{12}$

d $\frac{4}{5}-\frac{2}{3}=\frac{\square}{15}-\frac{\square}{15}=\frac{\square}{15}$

Change $\frac{4}{5}$ and $\frac{2}{3}$ like this $\frac{4\times 3}{5\times 3}=\frac{?}{15}, \frac{2\times 5}{3\times 5}=\frac{?}{15}$

e $\frac{1}{4}+\frac{2}{3}=\frac{\square}{12}+\frac{\square}{12}=\frac{\square}{12}$

f $\frac{1}{8}+\frac{5}{6}=\frac{\square}{24}+\frac{\square}{24}=\frac{\square}{24}$

3 Change these improper fractions into mixed numbers. Use the diagrams to help.

a $\frac{4}{3} = 1\frac{\square}{3}$

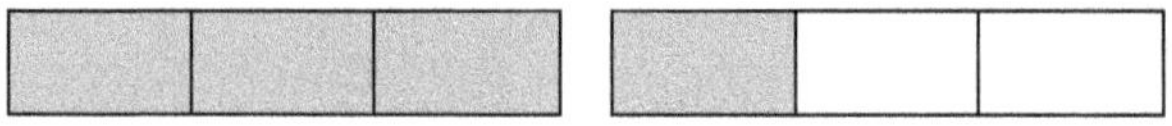

b $\frac{9}{5} = 1\frac{\square}{5}$

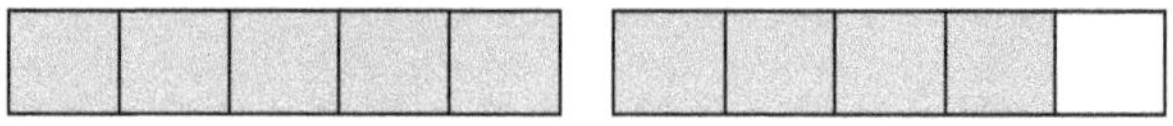

c $\frac{5}{4} = 1\frac{\square}{4}$

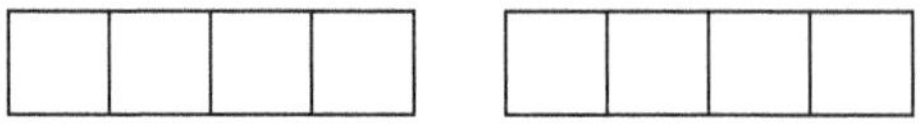

d $\frac{11}{6} = 1\frac{\square}{6}$

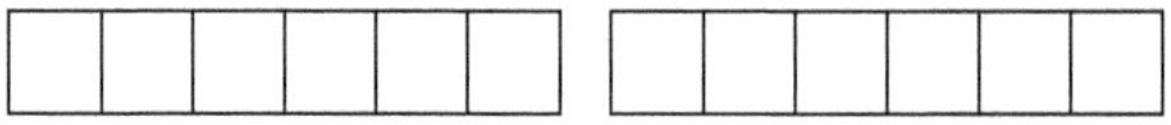

4 Work out these additions. Give each answer as a mixed number, using the diagrams to help. The first one has been started for you.

a $\frac{4}{5} + \frac{3}{5} = \frac{7}{5}, \frac{7}{5} = 1\frac{\square}{5}$

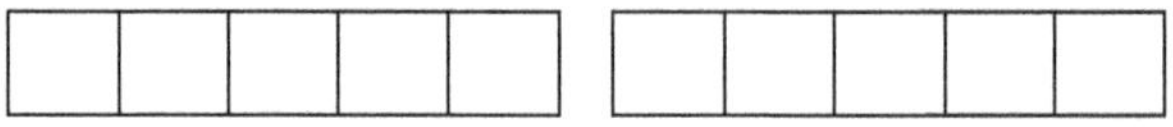

b $\frac{2}{9} + \frac{8}{9} = \frac{\square}{9}, \frac{\square}{9} = 1\frac{\square}{9}$

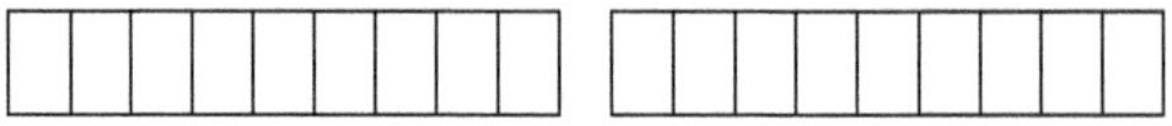

c $\frac{4}{5} + \frac{9}{10} = \frac{\square}{10} + \frac{9}{10} = \frac{\square}{10}, \frac{\square}{10} = 1\frac{\square}{10}$

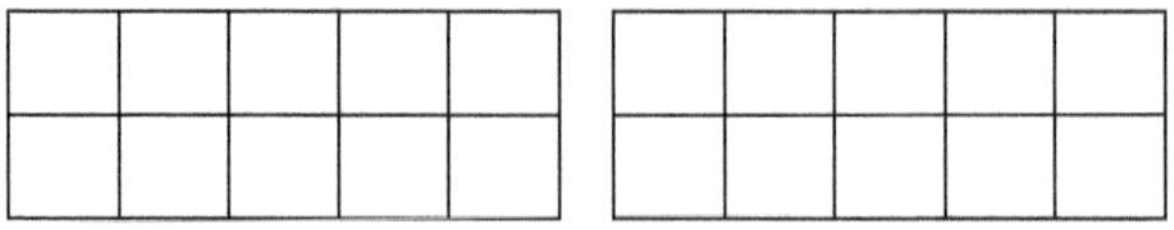

d $\frac{5}{6} + \frac{4}{5} = \frac{\square}{30} + \frac{\square}{30} = \frac{\square}{30}, \frac{\square}{30} = 1\frac{\square}{30}$

Now try Exercise 7.2 on page 67 of Coursebook 9.

7.3 Multiplying fractions

It is often easier to multiply an integer by a fraction by cancelling common factors first.
Look at the steps in this example:

1. Look at the denominator of the fraction, in this case it is 4. → $\frac{3}{4} \times 20$
2. 4 will go into 20 5 times, so rewrite 20 as 4 × 5. → $\frac{3}{\cancel{4}} \times \cancel{4} \times 5$
3. The ÷ 4 and × 4 cancel each other out.
4. Work out the remaining multiplication. → $3 \times 5 = 15$

1 Complete the working in these multiplications by cancelling common factors first.

a $\frac{2}{3} \times 12 = \frac{2}{3} \times 3 \times 4 = \ldots\ldots \times \ldots\ldots = \ldots\ldots$

3 is the common factor, so cross the 3s out.

b $\frac{3}{5} \times 20 = \frac{3}{5} \times \ldots\ldots \times \ldots\ldots = \ldots\ldots \times \ldots\ldots = \ldots\ldots$

Rewrite 20 as 5 × 4, then cancel the common factor.

c $\frac{5}{6} \times 18 = \frac{5}{6} \times \ldots\ldots \times \ldots\ldots = \ldots\ldots \times \ldots\ldots = \ldots\ldots$

Rewrite 18 as 6 × ?

d $\frac{4}{9} \times 27 = \frac{4}{9} \times \ldots\ldots \times \ldots\ldots = \ldots\ldots \times \ldots\ldots = \ldots\ldots$

Rewrite 27 as ? × ?

e $\frac{3}{4} \times 32 = \frac{3}{4} \times \ldots\ldots \times \ldots\ldots = \ldots\ldots \times \ldots\ldots = \ldots\ldots$

f $\frac{5}{8} \times 48 = \frac{5}{8} \times \ldots\ldots \times \ldots\ldots = \ldots\ldots \times \ldots\ldots = \ldots\ldots$

g $\frac{4}{7} \times 35 = \frac{4}{7} \times \ldots\ldots \times \ldots\ldots = \ldots\ldots \times \ldots\ldots = \ldots\ldots$

Sometimes you cannot divide the denominator into the integer, but you can still divide by a common factor. Look at this example:

$\frac{3}{4} \times 10$ ← **1** 4 will not divide exactly into 10, but 4 and 10 can both be divided by 2.

2 Rewrite 4 as 2 × 2 and 10 as 2 × 5. → $\frac{3}{2 \times \not{2}} \times \not{2} \times 5$ ← **3** One ÷ 2 and the × 2 cancel each other out.

4 Work out the remaining multiplication. → $\frac{3 \times 5}{2} = \frac{15}{2} = 7\frac{1}{2}$ ← **5** Write your answer as a mixed number.

2 Complete the working in these multiplications by cancelling common factors first.

a $\frac{1}{8} \times 20 = \frac{1}{4 \times 2} \times 4 \times 5 = \frac{\square \times \square}{\square} = \frac{\square}{2} = \square\frac{\square}{2}$

4 is the common factor, so cross them out.

b $\frac{3}{10} \times 25 = \frac{3}{\square \times \square} \times \ldots\ldots \times \ldots\ldots = \frac{\square \times \square}{\square} = \frac{\square}{2} = \square\frac{\square}{2}$

Rewrite 10 as 5 × 2 and 25 as 5 × 5.

c $\frac{3}{4} \times 14 = \frac{3}{\square \times \square} \times \ldots\ldots \times \ldots\ldots = \frac{\square \times \square}{\square} = \frac{\square}{\square} = \square\frac{\square}{\square}$

d $\frac{5}{9} \times 24 = \frac{5}{\square \times \square} \times \ldots\ldots \times \ldots\ldots = \frac{\square \times \square}{\square} = \frac{\square}{\square} = \square\frac{\square}{\square}$

Now try Exercise 7.3 on page 68 of Coursebook 9.

7.4 Dividing fractions

When you divide by a fraction, you turn the fraction upside down and multiply instead.

So the division $12 \div \frac{2}{3}$ becomes $12 \times \frac{3}{2}$.

1 Draw a line linking each division to its correct multiplication.
One has been done for you.

$12 \div \frac{3}{4}$	$12 \times \frac{4}{1}$
$12 \div \frac{3}{5}$	$12 \times \frac{4}{3}$
$12 \div \frac{1}{4}$	$12 \times \frac{3}{5}$
$12 \div \frac{5}{3}$	$12 \times \frac{3}{4}$
$12 \div \frac{4}{3}$	$12 \times \frac{5}{3}$

2 Complete the workings for these divisions. Remember to turn them into multiplications first, then cancel common factors.

a $12 \div \frac{2}{3} = 12 \times \frac{3}{2} = 6 \times 2 \times \frac{3}{2} =$ ...... × ...... = ...

2 is the common factor, so cross them out.

b $18 \div \frac{3}{4} = 18 \times \frac{\square}{\square} = 6 \times 3 \times \frac{\square}{\square} =$ ...... × ...... = ...

c $20 \div \frac{4}{7} = 20 \times \frac{\square}{\square} = 5 \times 4 \times \frac{\square}{\square} =$ ...... × ...... = ...

d $30 \div \frac{2}{3} = 30 \times \frac{\square}{\square} = 15 \times 2 \times \frac{\square}{\square} =$ ...... × ...... = ...

e $24 \div \frac{4}{5} = 24 \times \frac{\square}{\square} = \square \times 4 \times \frac{\square}{\square} =$ ...... × ...... = ...

3 Complete the workings for these divisions.

> Rewrite 15 as 5 × 3 and 6 as 3 × 2.
> 3 is the common factor, so cross them out.

a $15 \div \frac{6}{7} = 15 \times \frac{7}{6} = 5 \times 3 \times \frac{7}{3 \times 2} = \frac{5 \times 7}{2} = \frac{\square}{2} = \square\frac{\square}{2}$

b $12 \div \frac{8}{9} = 12 \times \frac{\square}{\square} = 3 \times 4 \times \frac{9}{\square \times \square} = \frac{3 \times 9}{\square} = \frac{\square}{2} = \square\frac{\square}{2}$

c $20 \div \frac{6}{5} = 20 \times \frac{\square}{\square} = 10 \times 2 \times \frac{5}{\square \times \square} = \frac{\square \times \square}{\square} = \frac{\square}{\square} = \square\frac{\square}{3}$

d $15 \div \frac{10}{13} = 15 \times \frac{\square}{\square} = 3 \times 5 \times \frac{13}{\square \times \square} = \frac{\square \times \square}{\square} = \frac{\square}{\square} = \square\frac{\square}{\square}$

Now try Exercise 7.4 on page 70 of Coursebook 9.

8 Constructions and Pythagoras' theorem

8.1 Using Pythagoras' theorem

Pythagoras' theorem is a rule that can only be used in right-angled triangles.

In a right-angled triangle, the longest side is called the **hypotenuse**.

The hypotenuse is always the side opposite the right angle.

Always label the hypotenuse a, and the other two sides b and c.

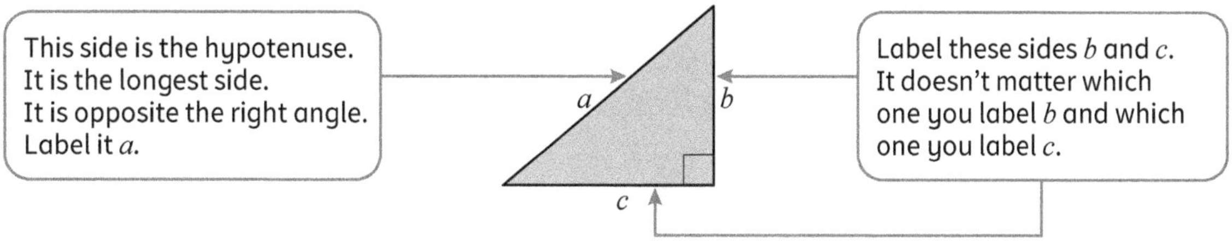

1 Label the sides of these triangles a, b and c. Always label the hypotenuse a.

a

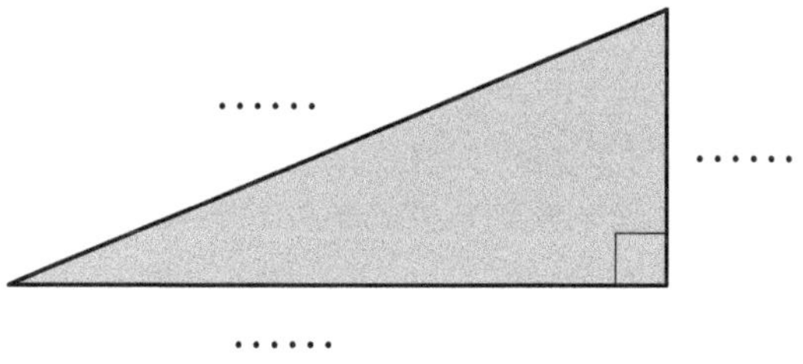

b

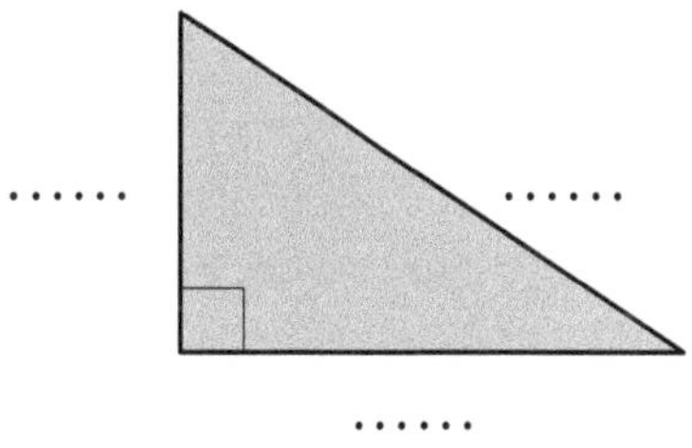

c

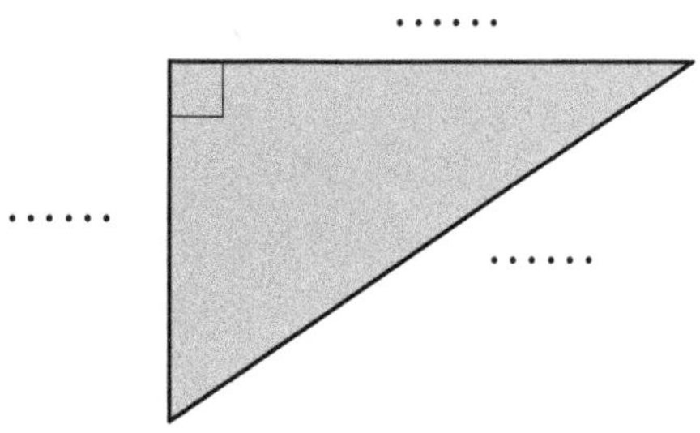

d

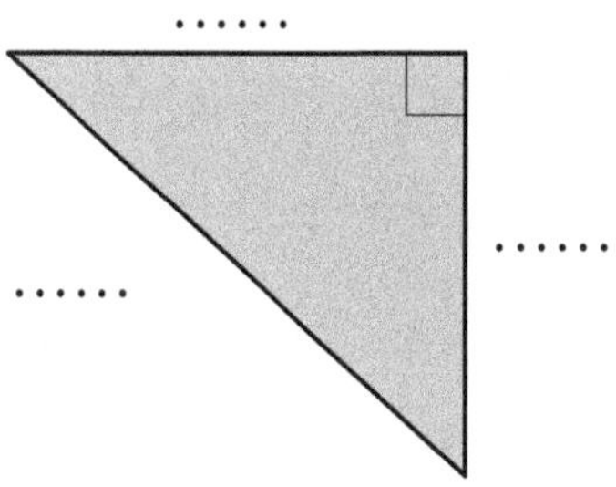

2 For each of these triangles, label the sides a, b and c. Then write down the values of a, b and c. The first one has been done for you.

a

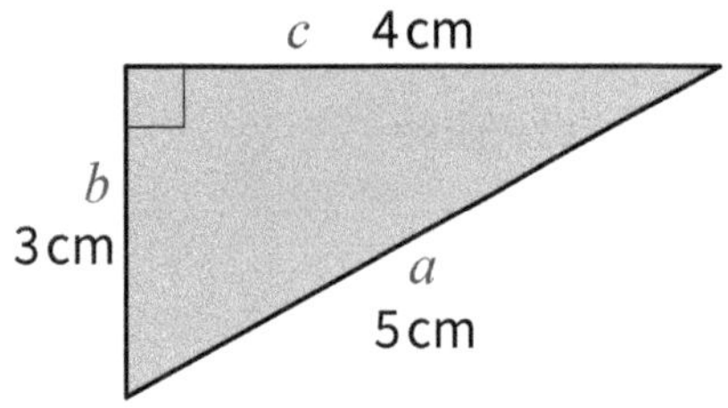

$a = 5$ cm $b = 3$ cm $c = 4$ cm

b

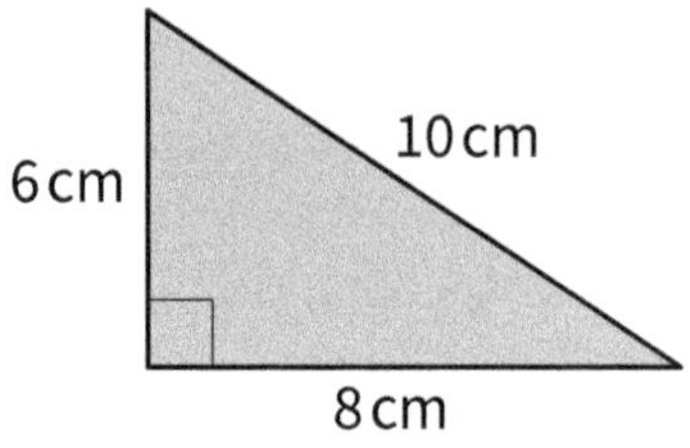

$a =$ ...... cm $b =$ ...... cm $c =$ ...... cm

c

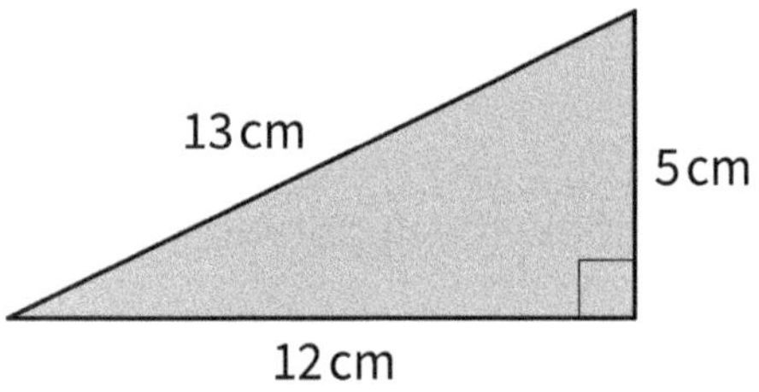

$a =$ ...... cm $b =$ ...... cm

$c =$ ...... cm

d

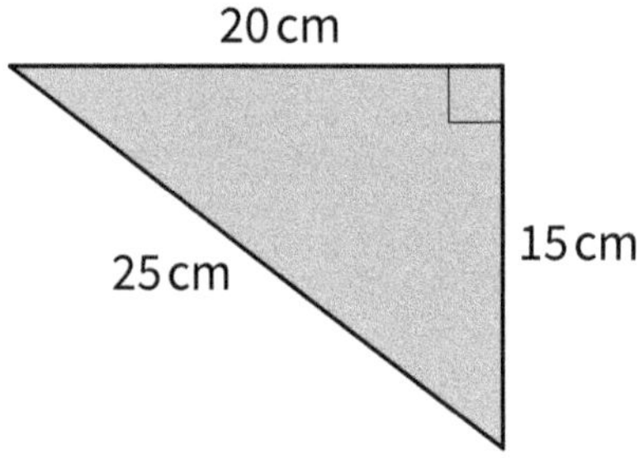

$a =$ ...... cm $b =$ ...... cm

$c =$ ...... cm

The formula for Pythagoras' theorem is $a^2 = b^2 + c^2$

Follow these steps to use Pythagoras' theorem:

① Label the sides a, b and c.

② Write down the values of the letters you know.

③ Write down Pythagoras' theorem.

④ Substitute the values of the letters you know.

⑤ Solve the equation.

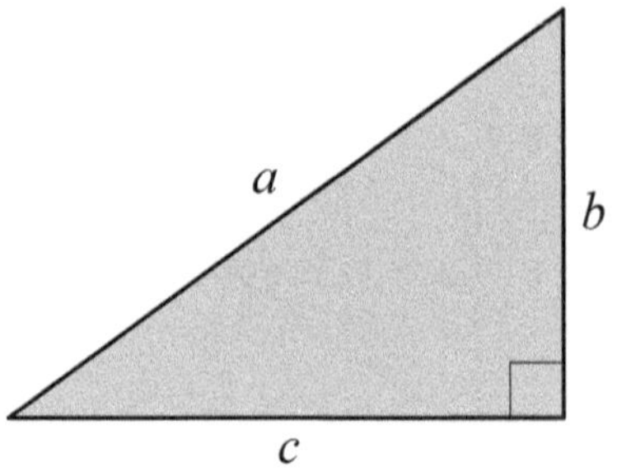

3 Complete the workings to find the length of the hypotenuse in each of these triangles.

a ① Label the sides a, b and c.

② $b = 9$ cm $\quad c = 12$ cm

③ $a^2 = b^2 + c^2$

④ $a^2 = 9^2 + 12^2$

⑤ $a^2 = 81 + 144$

$a^2 = 225$

$a = \sqrt{225} = \ldots\ldots$ cm

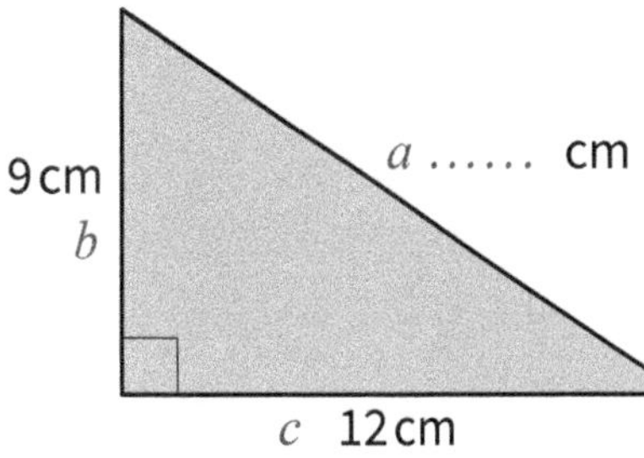

b ① Label the sides a, b and c.

② $b = \ldots\ldots$ cm $\quad c = \ldots\ldots$ cm

③ $a^2 = b^2 + c^2$

④ $a^2 = \ldots\ldots^2 + \ldots\ldots^2$

⑤ $a^2 = \ldots\ldots + \ldots\ldots$

$a^2 = \ldots\ldots$

$a = \sqrt{\ldots\ldots} = \ldots\ldots$ cm

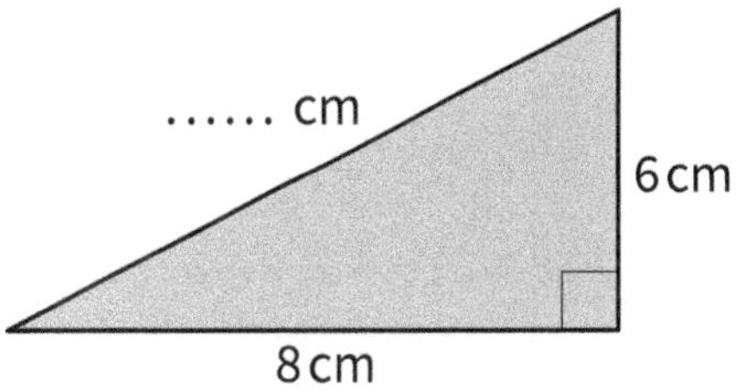

c ① Label the sides a, b and c.

② $b = \ldots\ldots$ cm $\quad c = \ldots\ldots$ cm

③ $a^2 = b^2 + c^2$

④ $a^2 = \ldots\ldots^2 + \ldots\ldots^2$

⑤ $a^2 = \ldots\ldots + \ldots\ldots$

$a^2 = \ldots\ldots$

$a = \sqrt{\ldots\ldots} = \ldots\ldots$ cm

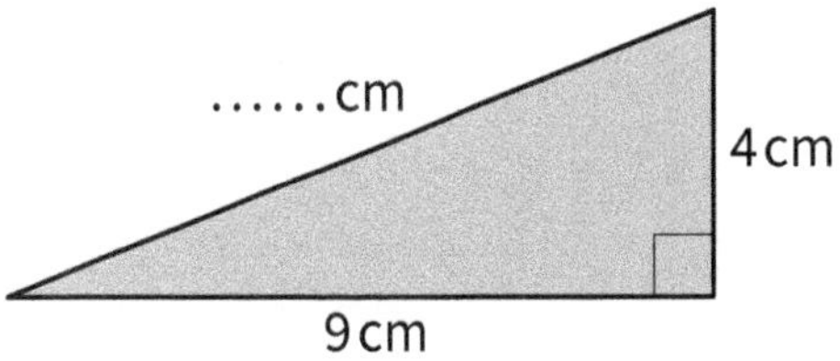

d ① Label the sides a, b and c.

② $b = \ldots\ldots$ cm $\quad c = \ldots\ldots$ cm

③ $a^2 = b^2 + c^2$

④ $a^2 = \ldots\ldots^2 + \ldots\ldots^2$

⑤ $a^2 = \ldots\ldots + \ldots\ldots$

$a^2 = \ldots\ldots$

$a = \sqrt{\ldots\ldots} = \ldots\ldots$ cm

Use a calculator to find the square root. Give your answer to 1 decimal place.

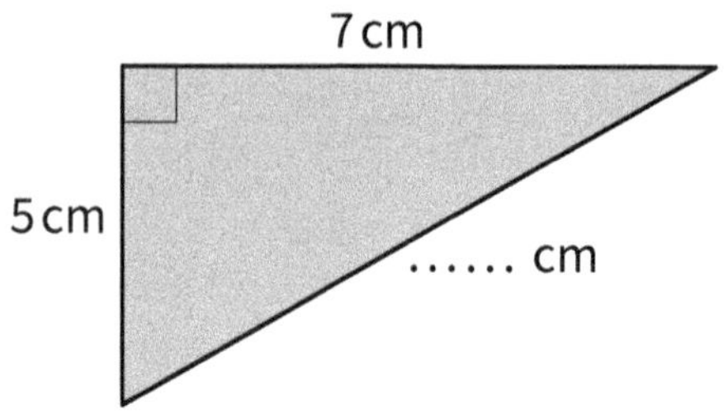

Now try Exercise 8.3 on page 82 of Coursebook 9.

9 Expressions and formulae

9.1 Simplifying algebraic expressions

The rules for indices with numbers can also be used for algebraic expressions.

When you multiply, you add the indices: $3^2 \times 3^3 = 3^{2+3} = 3^5$

It is the same for algebra: $x^2 \times x^3 = x^{2+3} = x^5$

1 Draw a line joining each rectangular card to its matching oval card. The first one has been done for you.

> $3 = 3^1$ and $x = x^1$.

Rectangular cards	Oval cards
$3^2 \times 3^4$	3^4
$3^3 \times 3^3$	x^7
3×3^3	3^6
$x^4 \times x^3$	x^8
$x^5 \times x$	3^6
$x^3 \times x^5$	x^6

2 Two of these statements are true and two are false. Write 'True' or 'False' next to each one. If the statement is false, write the correct answer.

a $x^2 \times x^4 = x^8$ ....

b $x \times x^3 = x^4$ ....

c $y^6 \times y = y^7$ ....

d $y^3 \times y^3 = y^9$ ....

3 Look at this method of simplifying $5x^2 \times 4x^3$

$5x^2 \times 4x^3 = 5 \times x^2 \times 4 \times x^3 = 5 \times 4 \times x^2 \times x^3 = 20 \times x^{2+3} = 20x^5$

Use the same method to simplify:

a $6x^2 \times 5x^3 =$ ....

b $4x^3 \times 3x^5 =$ ....

The rule is different for when you divide.

When dividing, you subtract the indices: $x^6 \div x^2 = x^{6-2} = x^4$

4 Complete the workings.

a $x^5 \div x^2 = x^{5-2} = x^{\dots\dots}$

b $x^7 \div x^4 = x^{\dots\dots - \dots\dots} = x^{\dots\dots}$

c $y^4 \div y^3 = y^{\dots\dots - \dots\dots} = y^{\dots\dots}$

d $y^6 \div y = y^{\dots\dots - \dots\dots} = y^{\dots\dots}$

5 Circle the correct answer for each of these divisions.

a $x^9 \div x^3 =$ x^3 x^6 x^{12}

b $x^{10} \div x^5 =$ x^{15} x^2 x^5

c $y^8 \div y =$ y^7 y^8 y^9

d $y^2 \div y^2 =$ y^4 y^1 y^0

Now try Exercise 9.1 on page 85 of Coursebook 9.

9.2 Constructing algebraic expressions

In algebraic expressions, you use letters to represent unknown numbers.

When you are asked to write an expression, think how you would write it with numbers first.

1 Add 2 to each of these numbers. Show your working. Parts a) and d) are done for you.

a) 4 $4 + 2 = 6$

4 + 2 can be simplified to 6.

b) 10   ....

c) 12   ....

d) x $x + 2$

$x + 2$ cannot be simplified so leave it as $x + 2$.

e) y ....

f) z ....

2 Subtract 3 from each of these numbers. Show your working.

a) 5   ....

b) 8   ....

c) 15   ....

d) x ....

e) y ....

f) z ....

3 Multiply each of these numbers by 5. Show your working.

a 2 ....

b 4 ....

c a ....

d b ....

$a \times 5$ can be simplified to $5a$.

4 Divide each of these numbers by 5. Show your working.

a 15 ....

b 30 ....

c a ....

d b ....

$a \div 5$ can be simplified to $\frac{a}{5}$.

5 I think of a number n...
Draw a line linking each of the statements to the correct expression.

I add 15	$15n$
I subtract 15	$3n + 5$
I multiply by 15	$n + 15$
I divide by 15	$5n - 3$
I subtract the number from 15	$\frac{n}{5} + 3$
I multiply by 3 then add 5	$n - 15$
I multiply by 5 then subtract 3	$\frac{n}{15}$
I divide by 5 then add 3	$15 - n$

Now try Exercise 9.2 on page 86 of Coursebook 9.

9.3 Substituting into expressions

When you substitute numbers into an expression or formula, you must use the correct order of operations:

B	I	D	M	A	S
Brackets	**I**ndices (powers)	**D**ivision	**M**ultiplication	**A**ddition	**S**ubtraction

1 Complete the workings to find the value of each expression when $x = 10$.

a $2x + 3$ $\quad 2 \times x + 3 = 2 \times 10 + 3$

$= \ldots\ldots + 3 = \ldots\ldots$

Work out the **M**ultiplication before the **A**ddition.

b $\frac{x}{2} - 4$ $\quad x \div 2 - 4 = 10 \div 2 - 4$

$= \ldots\ldots - 4 = \ldots\ldots$

Work out the **D**ivision before the **S**ubtraction.

c $4x^2$ $\quad 4 \times x^2 = 4 \times 10^2$

$= 4 \times \ldots\ldots = \ldots\ldots$

Work out the **I**ndices before the **M**ultiplication.

d $3(x + 2)$ $\quad 3 \times (x + 2) = 3 \times (10 + 2)$

$= 3 \times \ldots\ldots = \ldots\ldots$

Work out the **B**racket before the **M**ultiplication.

2 Draw a line linking each expression to the correct value when $a = 8$ and $b = 4$.

Remember, ab means $a \times b$.

$a + b$	32
$a - b$	$\frac{1}{2}$
ab	12
$\frac{a}{b}$	20
$\frac{b}{a}$	4
$2a + b$	2

3 Complete the workings.

Remember: + − → − and − − → +

a $3 + -2 = 3 - 2 = \ldots\ldots$

b $5 - -2 = 5 + 2 = \ldots\ldots$

c $4 \times -3 = \ldots\ldots$

d $-3 \times -5 = \ldots\ldots$

4 Complete the workings to find the values of the expressions when $x = 6$ and $y = -2$.

a $x + y = 6 + -2 = \ldots\ldots - \ldots\ldots = \ldots\ldots$

+ −2 is overall −2.

b $x - y = 6 - -2 = \ldots\ldots + \ldots\ldots = \ldots\ldots$

c $x^2 + y^2 = 6^2 + (-2)^2 = \ldots\ldots + \ldots\ldots = \ldots\ldots$

$(-2)^2$ is -2×-2.

d $3x + y = 3 \times 6 + -2 = \ldots\ldots - \ldots\ldots = \ldots\ldots$

e $x + 4y = 6 + 4 \times -2 = \ldots\ldots - \ldots\ldots = \ldots\ldots$

f $3x + 4y = 3 \times 6 + 4 \times -2 = \ldots\ldots - \ldots\ldots = \ldots\ldots$

Now try Exercise 9.3 on page 88 of Coursebook 9.

9.4 Deriving and using formulae

A formula is a mathematical rule that you can use to work out the value of something.

The formula for the area (A) of a rectangle is $A = lw$, where l is the length and w is the width.

A is the **subject of the formula** as it is written on its own.

1 You already know a lot of mathematical formulae. Match each rectangular card to the correct oval card.

Area of a triangle	$A = bh$
Volume of a cuboid	$C = \pi d$
Area of a parallelogram	$A = \pi r^2$
Circumference of a circle	$V = lbh$
Area of a trapezium	$A = \frac{1}{2}bh$
Area of a circle	$A = \frac{1}{2}(a + b)h$

2 **a** Work out the number of hours in each of these days.

i 1 day ...... **ii** 2 days ......

iii 3 days ...... **iv** d days ......

b The formula to work out the number of hours (H) in d days is $H = 24d$.
Complete the working to find the number of hours in 10 days.

$H = 24d = 24 \times d = 24 \times 10 =$ ......

Substitute $d = 10$ into the formula.

3 **a** Work out the number of days in each of these weeks.

i 1 week ...... ii 2 weeks ......

iii 3 weeks ...... iv w weeks ......

b The formula to work out the number of days (D) in w weeks is D = ...

Use your formula to find the number of days in 8 weeks.

....

4 **a** Work out the total number of days in:

i 1 week and 2 days ....

ii 3 weeks and 4 days ....

iii w weeks and d days ....

b The formula to work out the total number of days (T) in w weeks and d days is $T = 7w + d$.

Use the formula to work out the total number of days in:

i 2 weeks and 5 days ....

ii 6 weeks and 3 days ....

You can change the subject of a formula by rearranging the formula to get a different letter on its own.

5 Complete the working to make b the subject of these formulae. The first one has been done for you.

a $A = bh$ $A = b \times h$ swap sides: $b \times h = A$ reverse the ×: $b = \frac{A}{h}$

b $F = bg$ $F = b \times g$ swap sides: b × ...... = ... reverse the ×: $b = \frac{\square}{\square}$

c $T = mb$ $T = m \times b$ swap sides: ...... × ...... = ... reverse the ×: $b = \frac{\square}{\square}$

d $X = b + rt$ swap sides: $b + rt$ = ... reverse the +: b = X – ......

e $M = b - kn$ swap sides: b – ...... = ... reverse the –: b = ... + ...

Now try Exercise 9.4 on page 89 of Coursebook 9.

9.5 Factorising

When you **factorise** an expression, you do the opposite to expanding a bracket.

Expanding: $3(x + 8) = 3x + 24$

Factorising: $3x + 24 = 3(x + 8)$

1 Expand these brackets. Use the boxes to help if you want to. The first one has been done for you.

a $2(x + 6)$

×	x	6
2	$2x$	12

$2(x + 6) = 2x + 12$

b $3(x + 5)$

×	x	5
3		

$3(x + 5) =$ ...... + ...

c $5(y - 3)$

×	y	-3
5		

$5(y - 3) =$ ...... − ......

d $4(y - 7)$

×	y	-7
4		

$4(y - 7) =$ ...... − ......

2 Factorise these expressions. Use your answers to Question 1. The first one has been done for you.

a $2x + 12 = 2(x + 6)$

b $3x + 15 =$ ....

c $5y - 15 =$ ....

d $4y - 28 =$ ....

3 Complete these factorisations.

a $2x + 8 = 2(x +$ ......$)$

$2 \times x = 2x$ and $2 \times ? = 8$

b $3x + 9 = 3(x +$ ......$)$

c $5y - 30 = 5(y -$ ......$)$

d $8y + 16 = 8($...... + ...$)$

e $7y - 21 = 7($...... − ......$)$

4 Expand these brackets.

a $3(2x + 1) = 6x +$ ......

b $4(3x + 1) =$ ...... + ...

c $2(5y - 1) =$ ...... − ......

d $6(4y - 1) =$ ...... − ......

5 Use your answers to Question 4 to factorise these expressions.

a $6x + 3 =$ ......

b $12x + 4 =$ ......

c $10y - 2 =$ ......

d $24y - 6 =$ ......

6 Complete these factorisations.

a $4x + 6 = 2(2x +$ ......$)$

> 2 is the highest common factor of 4 and 6:
> $2 \times 2x = 4x$ and $2 \times ? = 6$

b $6x - 9 = 3($...... − ......$)$

> $3 \times ? = 6x$ and $3 \times ? = 9$

c $15x + 10 = 5($...... + ...$)$

> $5 \times ? = 15x$ and $5 \times ? = 10$

Now try Exercise 9.5 on page 91 of Coursebook 9.

9.6 Adding and subtracting algebraic fractions

An algebraic fraction is a fraction that contains a letter or letters.

$\frac{1}{4}$ and $\frac{2}{9}$ are not algebraic fractions.

$\frac{x}{4}$ and $\frac{2y}{9}$ and $\frac{x}{y}$ are all algebraic fractions.

You can add and subtract algebraic fractions using the same method as normal fractions.

1 Circle the algebraic fractions in this list.

$\frac{x}{2}$ $\frac{1}{3}$ $\frac{4}{5}$ $\frac{y}{9}$ $\frac{3x}{4}$ $\frac{7}{9}$ $\frac{11a}{12}$ $\frac{b}{c}$ $\frac{8}{15}$ $\frac{9g}{20}$ $\frac{1}{2d}$

2 Complete the answers to these fraction questions.

Write each answer in its simplest form.

a $\frac{1}{3}+\frac{1}{3}=\frac{\square}{3}$

b $\frac{1}{5}+\frac{2}{5}=\frac{\square}{\square}$

c $\frac{2}{7}+\frac{3}{7}=\frac{\square}{\square}$

d $\frac{1}{8}+\frac{3}{8}=\frac{4}{8}=\frac{\square}{\square}$

e $\frac{1}{9}+\frac{2}{9}=\frac{\square}{\square}=\frac{\square}{\square}$

f $\frac{3}{10}+\frac{3}{10}=\frac{\square}{\square}=\frac{\square}{\square}$

3 Complete the answers to these fraction questions.

Write each answer in its simplest form.

Use your answers to Question 2. The first one has been done for you.

a $\frac{x}{3}+\frac{x}{3}=\frac{2x}{3}$

b $\frac{x}{5}+\frac{2x}{5}=\frac{\square}{\square}$

c $\frac{2y}{7}+\frac{3y}{7}=\frac{\square}{\square}$

d $\frac{y}{8}+\frac{3y}{8}=\frac{4y}{8}=\frac{\square}{\square}$

e $\frac{m}{9}+\frac{2m}{9}=\frac{\square}{\square}=\frac{\square}{\square}$

f $\frac{3n}{10}+\frac{3n}{10}=\frac{\square}{\square}=\frac{\square}{\square}$

4 Work out the answers to these questions by finding a common denominator.

a $\frac{1}{4} + \frac{3}{8} = \frac{2}{8} + \frac{3}{8} = \frac{\square}{\square}$

$\frac{1}{4} = \frac{1 \times 2}{4 \times 2} = \frac{2}{8}$

b $\frac{1}{3} + \frac{2}{9} = \frac{\square}{\square} + \frac{\square}{\square} = \frac{\square}{\square}$

Change $\frac{1}{3}$ into $\frac{?}{9}$

c $\frac{2}{3} - \frac{1}{6} = \frac{\square}{\square} - \frac{\square}{\square} = \frac{\square}{\square} = \frac{\square}{\square}$

d $\frac{11}{12} - \frac{1}{6} = \frac{\square}{\square} - \frac{\square}{\square} = \frac{\square}{\square} = \frac{\square}{\square}$

5 Write down your answers to these questions. Use your answers to Question 4.

a $\frac{x}{4} + \frac{3x}{8} = \frac{\square}{\square}$

b $\frac{y}{3} + \frac{2y}{9} = \frac{\square}{\square}$

c $\frac{2p}{3} - \frac{p}{6} = \frac{\square}{\square}$

d $\frac{11b}{12} - \frac{b}{6} = \frac{\square}{\square}$

Now try Exercise 9.6 on page 93 of Coursebook 9.

10 Processing and presenting data

10.1 Calculating statistics

Here are the heights, in centimetres, of 25 plants:

10 10 10 10 10 11 11 11 12 12 12 12 13

13 14 14 14 14 14 14 14 14 15 15 15

Here are the 25 heights in a frequency table:

Height (cm)	10	11	12	13	14	15
Frequency	5	3	4	2	8	3

The shaded numbers show that two plants are 13 cm high.

To find the mean height, put the numbers in a table like this:

Height	**Frequency**	**Height × Frequency**	
10	5	50	10 × 5 = 50
11	3	33	
12	4	48	
13	2	26	
14	8	112	
15	3	45	
Total	25	314	Add the numbers in the columns.

The mean height is 314 ÷ 25 = 12.56 cm.

The mean does not have to be a whole number.

1 Here are the masses of the hand luggage of 20 passengers on a plane.

Mass (kg)	4	5	6	7	8
Frequency	1	4	5	8	2

Put the numbers in the table below. Use it to work out the mean mass.

Mass	**Frequency**	**Mass × Frequency**
4		
5		
6		
7		
8		
Total	20	

Mean mass = ... kg

2 Here are the number of people in 50 cars.

People in the car	1	2	3	4	5	6
Frequency	17	15	8	5	3	2

Work out the mean number of people. Use the table below.

People	**Frequency**	
Total		

Mean number of people = ...

3 This table shows the time that 60 people spend queuing to enter an exhibition.

Time (minutes)	5	6	7	8	9	10
Frequency	7	8	12	17	4	12

Work out the mean waiting time. Use the table below.

Mean waiting time = ... minutes.

4 Here are the marks of 40 students in a test.

Mark	14	15	16	17	18	19	20
Frequency	2	11	10	4	5	3	5

Work out the mean mark. Use the table below.

The mean mark is ......

Here are the heights of the plants from the first example again.

Height (cm)	10	11	12	13	14	15
Frequency	5	3	4	2	8	3

The **mode** is 14 cm because it is the most common height.

14 cm has the highest frequency.

5 Find the mode for each of these tables from the previous questions.

a

Mass (kg)	4	5	6	7	8
Frequency	1	4	5	8	2

The mode is ...... kg.

b

People in the car	1	2	3	4	5	6
Frequency	17	15	8	5	3	2

The mode is ...... people.

c

Time (minutes)	5	6	7	8	9	10
Frequency	7	8	12	17	4	12

The mode is ...... minutes.

d

Mark	14	15	16	17	18	19	20
Frequency	2	11	10	4	5	3	5

The mode is ...... marks.

Now try Exercise 10.1 on page 98 of Coursebook 9.

10.2 Using statistics

Here are the ages of five boys:	13	14	11	14	10			
To find the median, write the ages in order:	10	11	13	14	14			

The median is the age in the middle. The median age of the boys is 13 years.

To find the mean, add the ages and divide by 5: $(13 + 14 + 11 + 14 + 10) \div 5 = 12.4$
The mean age of the boys is 12.4 years.

Here are the ages of eight girls	11	8	13	13	11	15	10	13
Write them in order:	8	10	11	11	13	13	13	15

The middle is half way between 11 and 13. The median age for the girls is 12 years.

The mean age of the girls is 11.75 years. $(11 + 8 + 13 + 13 + 11 + 15 + 10 + 13) \div 8 = 11.75$

1 Here are the masses, in kg, of some men and women:

Men	56	62	69	58	67		
Women	47	40	51	48	39	50	40

The median mass of the men is 62 kg. The mean mass of the men is 62.4 kg.
Fill in the averages.

a The median mass of the women is ...... kg.

b The mean mass of the women is ...... kg.

Circle the correct words and fill in the masses.

c The men's median mass is **greater/less** than the women's median mass by ...... kg.

d The men's mean mass is **greater/less** than the women's mean mass by ...... kg.

2 Here are the heights, in centimetres, of some young children:

Girls	97	93	104	92	
Boys	90	102	96	92	91

The median height of the boys is 92 cm. The mean height of the boys is 94.2 cm.
Fill in the averages.

a The median height of the girls is ...... cm.

b The mean height of the girls is ...... cm.

Circle the correct words and fill in the heights.

c The girls' median height is **greater/less** than the boys' median height by ...... cm.

d The girls' mean height is **greater/less** than the boys' mean height by ...... cm.

3 Here are the times, in seconds, for the runners in two races:

Race 1:	45	43	59	55	48	50		
Race 2:	42	56	53	58	51	48	50	50

The median time for race 1 is 49 seconds. The mean time for race 1 is 50 seconds.
Fill in the averages.

a Median time for race 2 is ...... seconds.

b Mean time for race 2 is ...... seconds.

c Which race had the quicker median time? ......

d Which race had the quicker mean time? ......

4 Here are the times, in minutes, some children take to get to school:

Class X:	15	20	25	40	20	25	45	15	20	20
Class Y:	30	10	40	45	25	30				

The median time for class X is 20 minutes. The mean time for class X is 24.5 minutes.
Find these average times.

a The median time for class Y is ...... minutes.

b The mean time for class Y is ...... minutes.

c Write two sentences comparing the average times for class X and class Y.

....

....

....

....

Now try Exercise 10.2 on page 100 of Coursebook 9.

11 Percentages

11.1 Using mental methods

You can change simple percentages to fractions.

1 Write these percentages as fractions. The first one has been done for you.

a. $50\% = \frac{1}{2}$ b. $25\% = \ldots\ldots$ c. $75\% = \ldots\ldots$

d. $10\% = \ldots\ldots$ e. $20\% = \ldots\ldots$ f. $1\% = \ldots\ldots$

2 Complete this diagram.

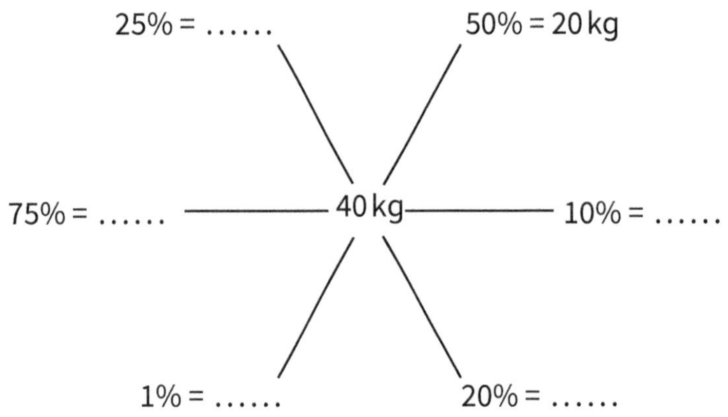

3 Complete this diagram.

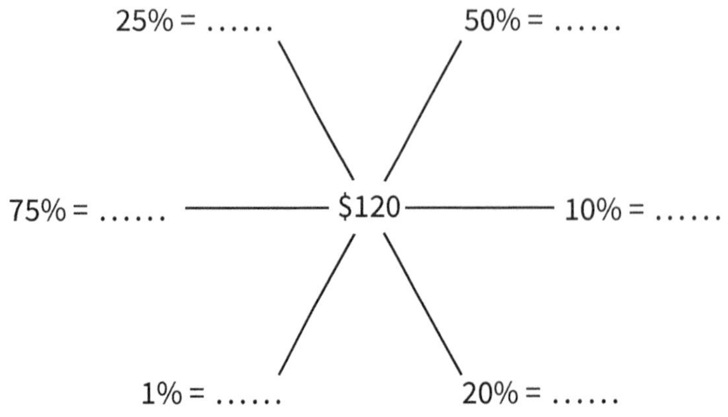

4 Complete this diagram.

25% = ...   50% = ...

75% = ... $6   10% = ...

1% = ...   20% = ...

If you can find 50%, 25% and 10%, you can use them to find other percentages.

Suppose 100% is 60 g.

50% of 60 g = 30 g   25% of 60 g = 15 g   10% = 6 g

Then 60% = 50% + 10% = 30 g + 6 g = 36 g

and 15% = 25% – 10% = 15 g – 6 g = 9 g

5 Complete this table.

	80 kg	24 m	$240	$5	30 hours
50%	40 kg				
10%	8 kg				
60%	48 kg				

6 Complete this table.

	20 km	$44	$6	64 cm	160 kg
25%	5 km				
10%	2 kg				
35%	7 kg				

7 Complete this table.

	50%	25%	10%	75%	60%	85%
$400	$200	$100	$40	$300	$240	$340
$80						
$220						

8 Complete this table.

	50%	25%	75%	10%	65%	15%
60 kg						
300 cm						
420 g						

65% = 75% − 10%

Now try Exercise 11.1 on page 104 of Coursebook 9.

11.2 Percentage changes

The price of a computer is \$600.
The price increases by 10%.
10% of \$600 = \$60.
The new price is \$600 + \$60 = \$660.

1 Some prices are increased by 10%. Complete this table.

Original price	10% increase	New price
\$600	\$60	\$660
\$40		
\$70		
\$430		
\$2500		

2 The height of a plant increases by 25%. Complete this table.

Original height	25% increase	New height
32 cm	8 cm	
12 cm		
28 cm		
44 cm		
124 cm		

3 The mass of some animals increases by 20%. Complete this table.

Original mass	10%	20%	New mass
12 kg	1.2 kg	2.4 kg	14.4 kg
20 kg			
15 kg			
44 kg			

You can work out decreases in the same way.
The price of a computer is \$600.
The price decreases by 20%.
20% of \$600 = \$120.
The new price is \$600 – \$120 = \$480.

4 Some prices are decreased by 25%. Complete this table.

Original price	25% decrease	New price
\$32	\$8	\$24
\$80		
\$44		
\$280		
\$620		

You can write an increase as a percentage.
A price increases from \$60 to \$66.
The increase is \$6.
The increase is 10% of \$60.

\$6 is 10% of \$60.

5 Fill in the missing numbers.

a A price increases from \$40 to \$44. The increase is \$......
The increase is ......% of \$40.

b A price increases from \$40 to \$50. The increase is \$......
The increase is ......% of \$40.

c A price increases from \$40 to \$60. The increase is \$......
The increase is ......% of \$40.

6 Fill in the missing numbers.

a A price increases from \$80 to \$120. The increase is \$......
The increase is ......% of \$80.

b A price increases from \$80 to \$100. The increase is \$......
The increase is ......% of \$80.

c A price increases from \$80 to \$88. The increase is \$......
The increase is ......% of \$80.

7 Fill in the missing numbers.

a A height increases from 120 cm to 150 cm. The increase is ...... cm

The increase is ......% of 120 cm.

b A height increases from 120 cm to 132 cm. The increase is ...... cm

The increase is ......% of 120 cm.

c A height increases from 120 cm to 180 cm. The increase is ...... cm

The increase is ......% of 120 cm.

8 Fill in the missing numbers.

a A price increases from \$5 to \$7.50. The increase is \$......

The increase is ......% of \$5.

b A price increases from \$5 to \$5.50. The increase is \$......

The increase is ......% of \$5.

c A price increases from \$5 to \$6.25. The increase is \$......

The increase is ......% of \$5.

Now try Exercise 11.3 on page 106 of Coursebook 9.

12 Tessellations, transformations and loci

12.1 Tessellating shapes

A **tessellation** is a pattern made of identical shapes that fit together without gaps or overlaps.

1 On each of the grids below, add six more shapes to each tessellation.

Make sure that the extra shapes you add to each pattern are identical to the other shapes.

Remember, there must be no gaps between shapes. The shapes must not overlap.

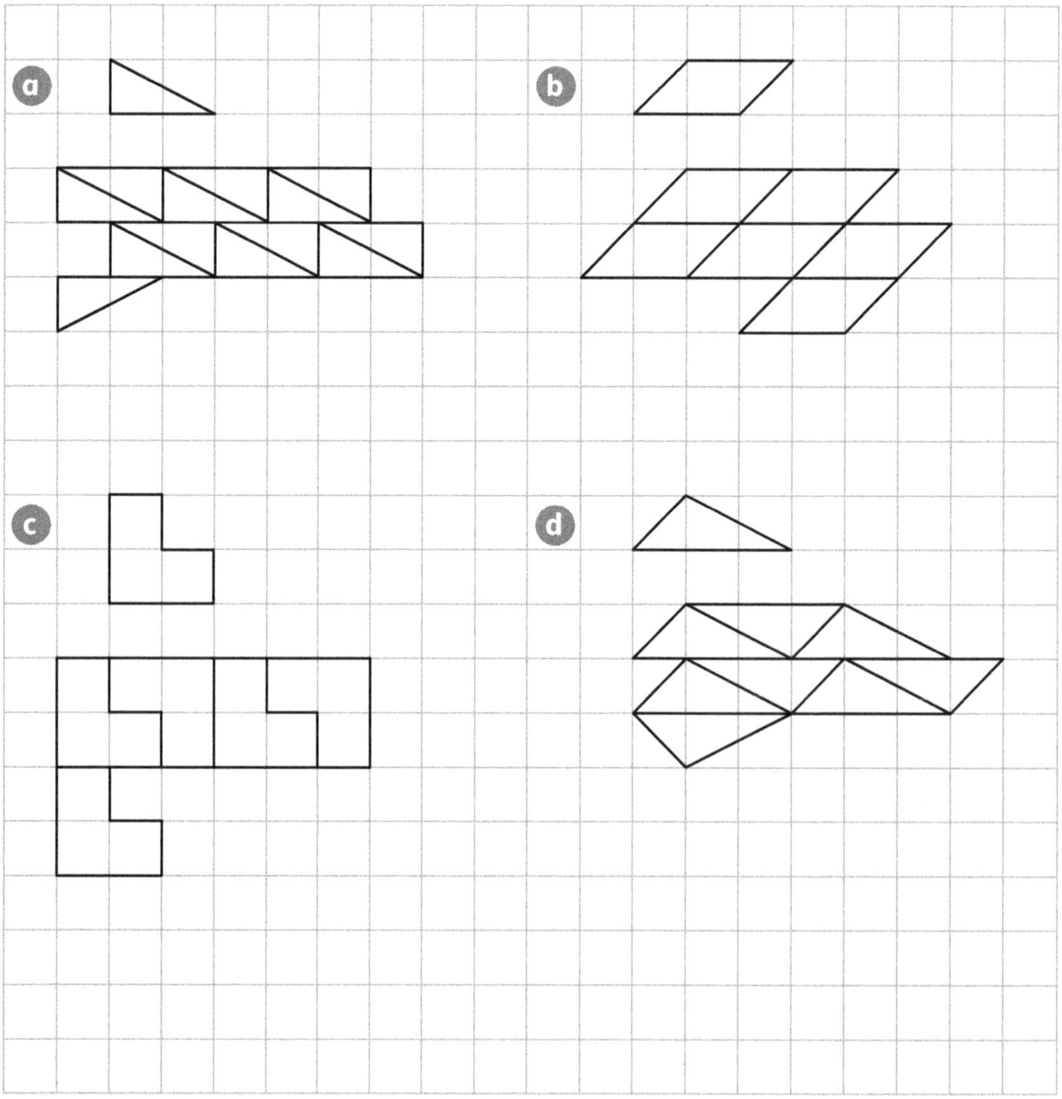

Now try Exercise 12.1 on page 112 of Coursebook 9.

12.2 Solving transformation problems

When you translate a shape on a coordinate grid, you can use a **column vector** to describe its movement.

The column vector $\begin{pmatrix}1\\2\end{pmatrix}$ means 'Move the shape 1 unit right and 2 units up'.

The column vector $\begin{pmatrix}-1\\-2\end{pmatrix}$ means 'Move the shape 1 unit left and 2 units down'.

– means move left ←	(top number)	→ + means move right
– means move down ←	(bottom number)	→ + means move up

1 Draw a line linking each column vector to the correct description. The first one has been done for you.

$\begin{pmatrix}2\\3\end{pmatrix}$	Move the shape 2 units left and 3 units down
$\begin{pmatrix}2\\-3\end{pmatrix}$	Move the shape 3 units right and 2 units up
$\begin{pmatrix}-2\\-3\end{pmatrix}$	Move the shape 2 units left and 3 units up
$\begin{pmatrix}-3\\2\end{pmatrix}$	Move the shape 2 units right and 3 units up
$\begin{pmatrix}-2\\3\end{pmatrix}$	Move the shape 3 units left and 2 units up
$\begin{pmatrix}3\\2\end{pmatrix}$	Move the shape 2 units right and 3 units down

2 Fill in the missing numbers and words in these statements.

a The column vector $\begin{pmatrix}4\\5\end{pmatrix}$ means move the shape ...... units right and 5 units ......

b The column vector $\begin{pmatrix}-1\\6\end{pmatrix}$ means move the shape 1 unit ...... and ...... units up.

c The column vector $\begin{pmatrix}2\\-4\end{pmatrix}$ means move the shape 2 units ...... and 4 units ......

3 Translate the rectangles using the given column vectors.

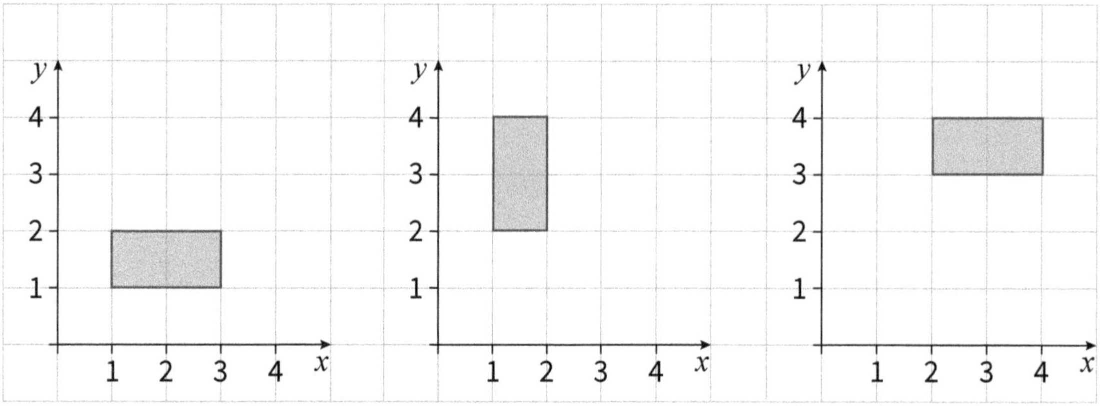

a $\begin{pmatrix} 1 \\ 2 \end{pmatrix}$

b $\begin{pmatrix} 2 \\ -1 \end{pmatrix}$

c $\begin{pmatrix} -1 \\ -2 \end{pmatrix}$

When you reflect a shape on a coordinate grid, you need to know the equation of the mirror line.

The diagram shows the lines with equation $y = 2$ and $x = -3$.

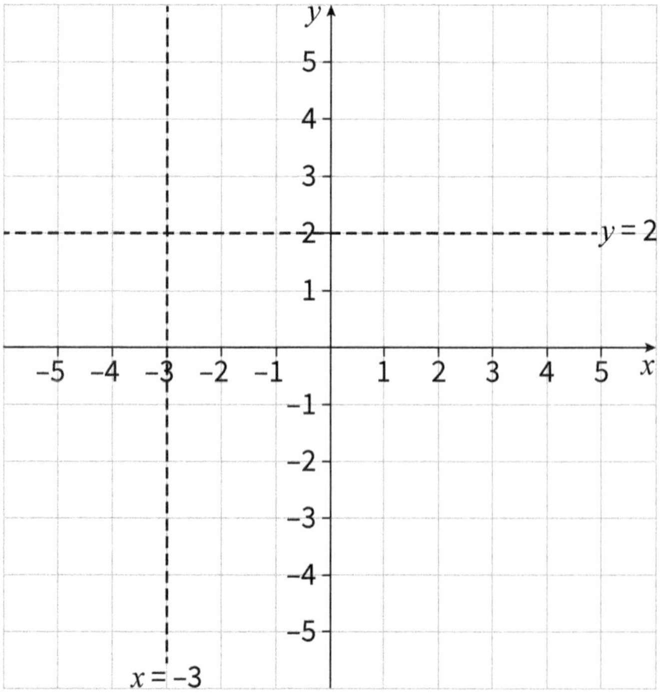

All horizontal lines have the equation y = 'a number'; all vertical lines have the equation x = 'a number'.

4 On the diagram above, draw the lines with the following equations.

Make sure you write the equation of the line next to each one.

a $x = 1$

b $x = -5$

c $y = 4$

d $y = -3$

5 Reflect each shape in the given mirror line.

Draw the mirror line first. Reflect each shape one corner at a time, then join the points with straight lines.

a

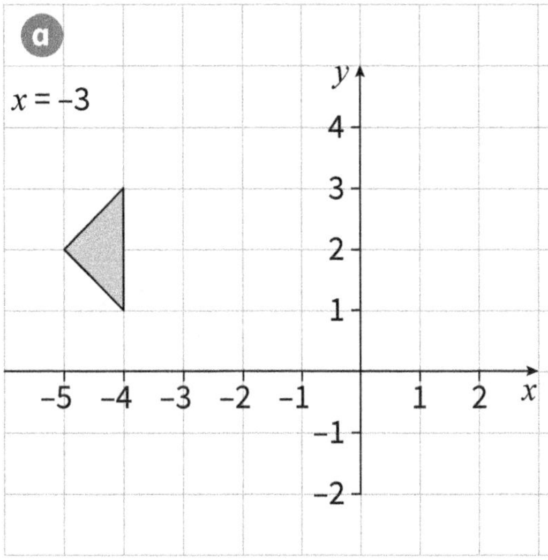

b

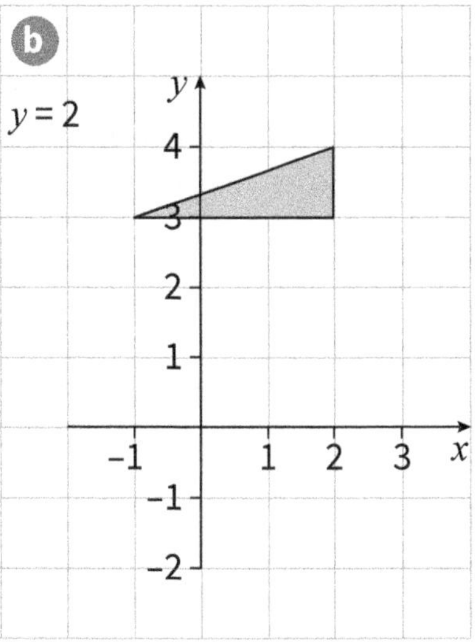

6 On the grid, write the equations of each of the mirror lines shown. One has been done for you.

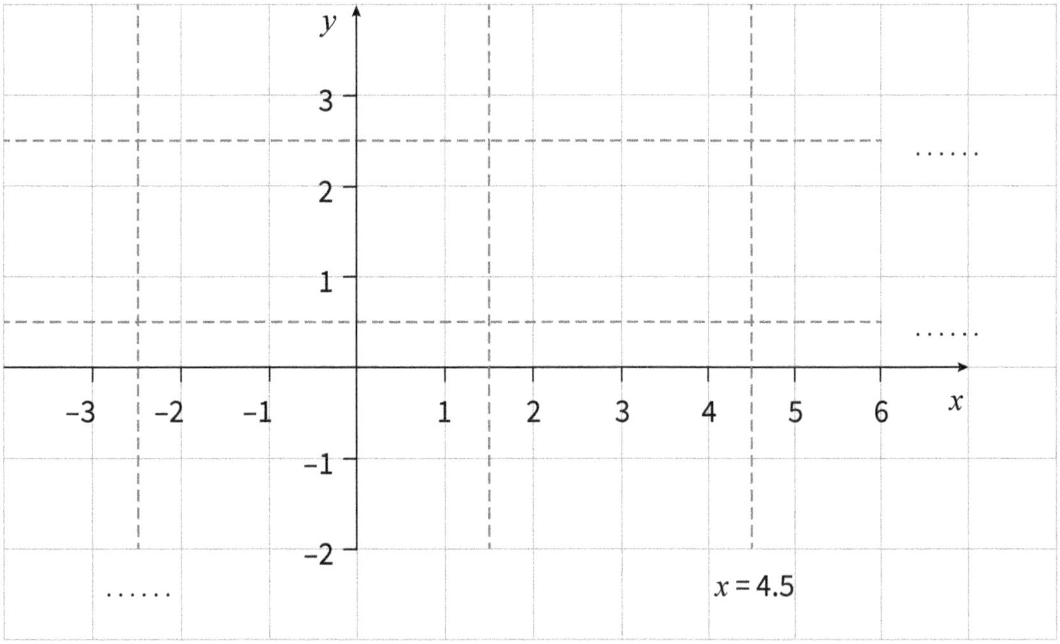

Now try Exercise 12.2 on page 114 of Coursebook 9.

12.3 Enlarging shapes

An **enlargement** of a shape is a copy of the shape that is either bigger or smaller than the original.

You enlarge a shape using a **scale factor** and a **centre of enlargement**.

1 Complete these enlargements using a scale factor of 2 and the centre of enlargement given. X marks the position of the centre of enlargement. One side of each triangle has been drawn for you.

Follow these steps:

Step 1: Count the number of squares from the centre of enlargement to the nearest corner of the triangle. Multiply this number by 2 to find the new distance from the centre of enlargement. Plot this point.

Step 2: Count the length and height, in squares, of the triangle. Multiply both of these by 2 to find the new length and height. Draw the enlarged triangle from the corner you have already plotted.

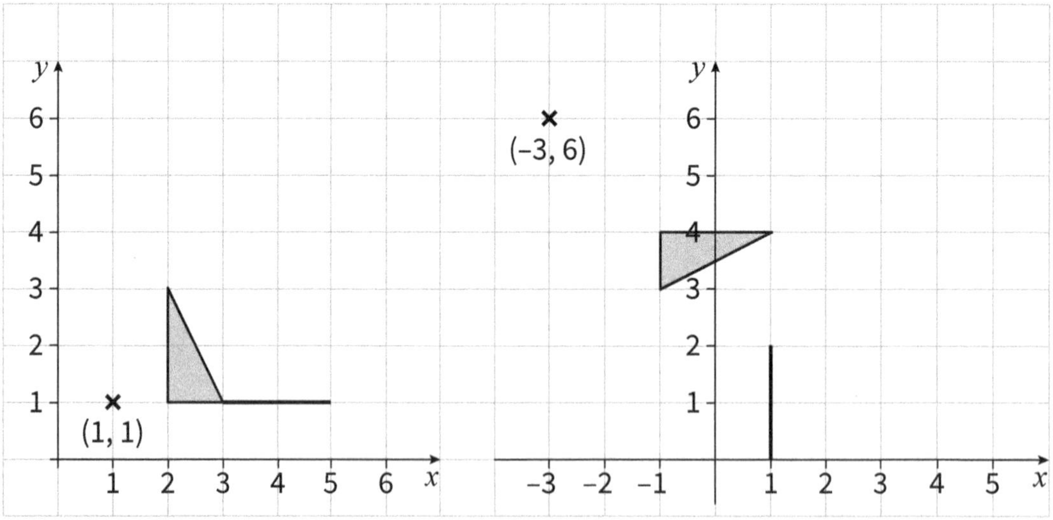

2 Complete these enlargements using a scale factor of 3 and the centre of enlargement given.

X marks the position of the centre of enlargement. The dot shows the position of one of the corners of the enlarged shape.

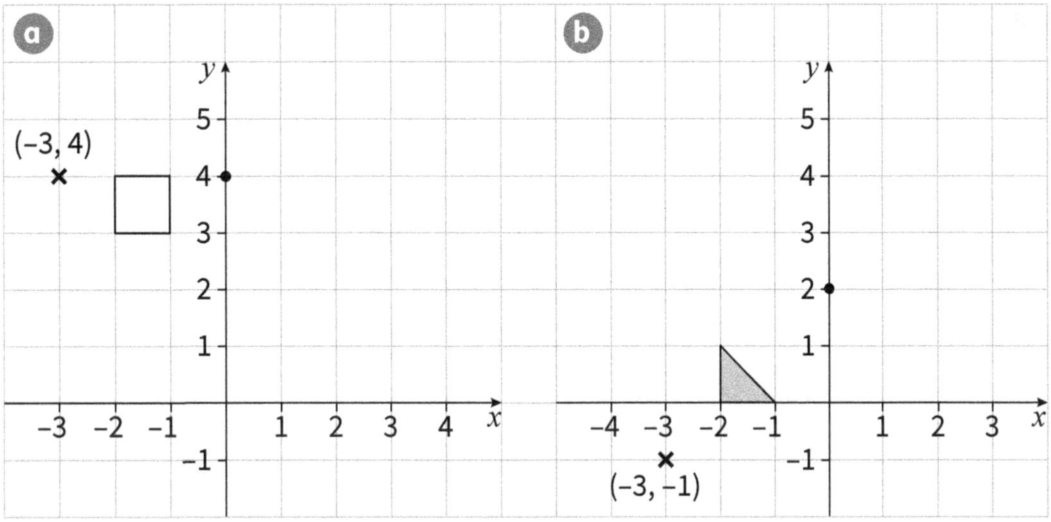

Now try Exercise 12.4 on page 120 of Coursebook 9.

13 Equations and inequalities

13.1 Solving linear equations

Suppose $x = 6$.

You can use this fact to work out other expressions.

Check the following are correct:

$x + 5 = 11$ $\quad$ $x - 4 = 2$ $\quad$ $3x = 18$

3x means 3 × x.

$2x - 5 = 7$ $\quad$ $4(x - 2) = 16$

Work out a bracket first, so work out $x - 2$ first and then multiply by 4.

1 Find the missing values when $x = 5$.

a $x + 6 =$ ......

b $x - 4 =$ ......

c $3x =$ ......

2 Complete the following.

$x = 3$ $\quad$ $2x =$ ...... $\quad$ $2x + 5 =$ ...... $\quad$ $4x - 1 =$ ......

3 Complete the following.

$x = 5$ $\quad$ $3x =$ ...... $\quad$ $3x - 2 =$ ...... $\quad$ $3x + 8 =$ ......

4 Complete the following.

$x = 4$ $\quad$ $x + 3 =$ ...... $\quad$ $2(x + 3) =$ ...... $\quad$ $4(x + 3) =$ ......

5 Complete the following.

$x = 8$ $\quad$ $x - 6 =$ ...... $\quad$ $4(x - 6) =$ ...... $\quad$ $10(x - 6) =$ ......

6 Fill in the missing numbers.

$4(x + 2) = ...$

$4(x - 1) = ...$ $x + 2 = ...$ $2x + 5 = ...$

$x - 1 = ...$ $2x = ...$

$x = 6$

$4x = ...$ $3x = ...$

$4x - 10 = ...$ $x - 4 = ...$ $3x - 6 = ...$

$5(x - 4) = ...$

You can also reverse the arrows to find the value of x.

$3x + 5 = 29$ → (Subtract 5) → $3x = 24$ → (Divide by 3) → $x = 8$

Check the answer: when $x = 8$, $3x + 5 = 29$

7 Complete these diagrams.

a $2x + 6 = 20$ → $2x = ...$ → $x = ...$

b $3x - 2 = 13$ → $3x = ...$ → $x = ...$

c $5x + 1 = 31$ → $5x = ...$ → $x = ...$

d $2(x - 2) = 20$ → $x - 2 = ...$ → $x = ...$

e $3(x + 5) = 33$ → $x + 5 = ...$ → $x = ...$

f $5(x - 4) = 35$ → $x - 4 = ...$ → $x = ...$

8 Fill in the missing numbers.

$3(x-2)=15$ ⟵ $x-2=$ ...... ⟵ $x=$ ...... ⟶ $3x=$ ...... ⟶ $3x-2=$ ......

9 Fill in the missing numbers.

$4(x+3)=$ ...... ⟵ $x+3=$ ...... ⟵ $x=$ ...... ⟶ $4x=$ ...... ⟶ $4x+3=27$

Now try Exercise 13.1 on page 125 of Coursebook 9.

13.2 Trial and improvement

You need a calculator for this section.

$3^2 = 3 \times 3 = 9$ $\quad$ $9^2 = 9 \times 9 = 81$

Read 3^2 as 'three squared' and 9^2 as 'nine squared'.

Here is an equation: $x^2 + 2x = 48$

You can try to guess a solution:

Try $x = 4$ $\quad$ Then $x^2 + 2x = 4^2 + 2 \times 4 = 16 + 8 = 24$ $\quad$ That is too small.

Try $x = 8$ $\quad$ Then $x^2 + 2x = 8^2 + 2 \times 8 = 64 + 16 = 80$ $\quad$ That is too large.

Try $x = 6$ $\quad$ Then $x^2 + 2x = 6^2 + 2 \times 6 = 36 + 12 = 48$ $\quad$ That is correct.

The solution is $x = 6$

It is a good idea to put your trials in a table like this:

You can use a calculator for these calculations.

x	$x^2 + 2x$	
4	24	too small
8	80	too large
6	48	solution

The solution is $x = 6$.

This method is called **trial and improvement**.

1 Solve the equation $x^2 + x = 72$. Put your trials in this table.

x	$x^2 + x$	
5	30	too small
6		
9		
8		

The solution is $x = \ldots\ldots$

2 Solve the equation $x^2 - 2x = 24$. Put your trials in this table.

x	$x^2 - 2x$	
9	63	too large

You choose the numbers to try.

The solution is $x =$ ......

3 Solve the equation $x^2 + 4x = 165$. Put your trials in this table.

x	$x^2 + 4x$	

The solution is $x =$ ......

4 Solve the equation $x^2 - 5x = 50$. Put your trials in this table.

x	$x^2 - 5x$	

The solution is $x =$ ......

Sometimes you cannot find an exact solution. Here is a table to solve the equation $x^2 + x = 18$:

x	$x^2 + x$	
3	12	too small
4	20	too large

The solution is between 3 and 4.
Try 3.5, which is half way between.

3.5	15.75	too small

It is between 3.5 and 4. Choose numbers to try:

3.8	18.24	too large
3.7	17.39	too small

You can stop there. The solution is between 3.7 and 3.8.

5 Use the table to try and solve the equation $x^2 + x = 45$ in the same way.

Start with 6 and 7 and 6.5 then decide what to try next.

x	$x^2 + x$	
6		too small
7		
6.5		

The solution is between ..... and ......

6 Use the table to try and solve the equation $x^2 + 2x = 31$.

Start with 4 and then decide what to try next.

x	$x^2 + 2x$	
4	24	

The solution is between ...... and ......

7 Use the table to try and solve the equation $x^2 - x = 88$.

x	$x^2 - x$	

The solution is between ...... and ......

Now try Exercise 13.5 on page 131 of Coursebook 9.

14 Ratio and proportion

14.1 Comparing and using ratios

You can write any ratio in the form 1 : n, where n is a number.

This is useful when you compare ratios. Look at this example.

Harry and Misha make grey paint by mixing white and black paint.

Harry mixes white to black in the ratio 2 : 8

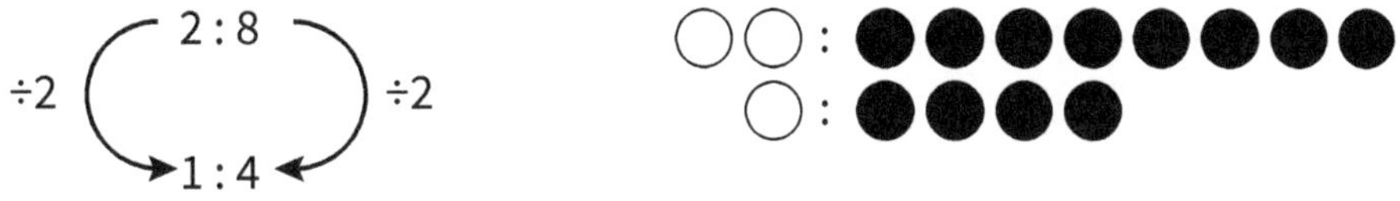

Misha mixes white to black in the ratio 3 : 9

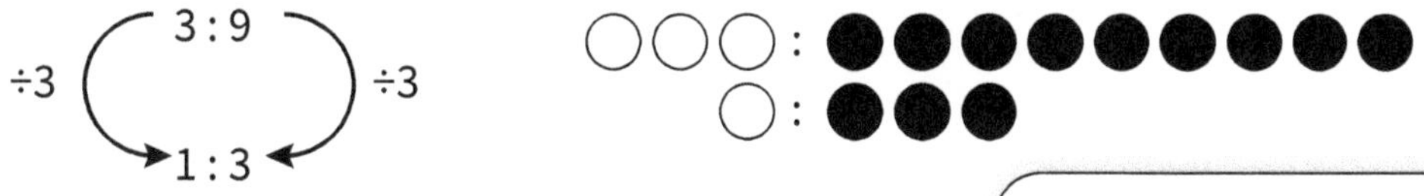

Harry has the darker paint because he has four blacks for every white, while Misha only has three blacks for every white.

Think of Harry mixing four tins of black with one tin of white, and Misha mixing three tins of black with one tin of white.

1 Harsha and Oditi make pink paint by mixing white and red paint. Harsha mixes white and red in the ratio 3 : 6. Oditi mixes white and red in the ratio 4 : 12.

Complete the working to find out who has the darker paint.

Harsha

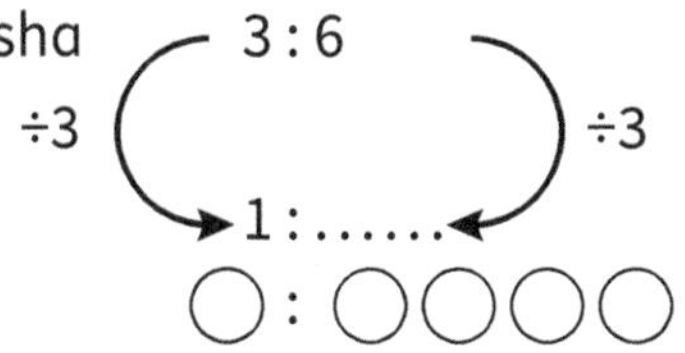

Oditi

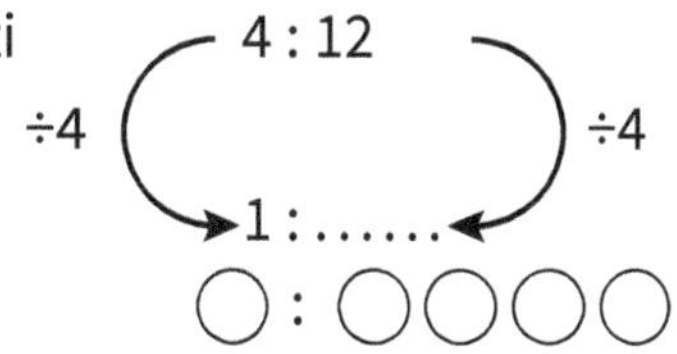

.... has the darker paint.

Colour in the circles that you need for the red paint, to help you compare.

2 Jake and Razi make light blue paint by mixing white and blue paint. Jake mixes white and blue in the ratio 2 : 5. Razi mixes white and blue in the ratio 4 : 13.

Complete the working to find out who has the darker paint.

Jake

2 : 5

÷2 ÷2

1 : .....

○ : ○○○○

Razi

4 : 13

÷4 ÷4

1 : .....

○ : ○○○○

.... has the darker paint.

Colour in the circles that you need for the blue paint, to help you compare.

Now try Exercise 14.1 on page 136 of Coursebook 9.

14.2 Solving problems

Two quantities are in direct proportion when their ratios stay the same as they increase or decrease.

You can use direct proportion to solve problems like the one below.

A pack of 4 kitchen rolls costs \$1.80. A pack of 6 kitchen rolls costs \$2.52.

Which pack is the better value for money?

Find the cost of one kitchen roll first, then compare prices.

4 kitchen rolls costs \$1.80, so 1 costs \$1.80 ÷ 4 = \$0.45 or 45 cents.

6 kitchen rolls costs \$2.52, so 1 costs \$2.52 ÷ 6 = \$0.42 or 42 cents

The 6-pack is better value as it costs 3 cents less per kitchen roll.

1 A pack of 6 toilet rolls costs \$4.02. A pack of 10 toilet rolls costs \$6.80.

Which pack is the better value for money?
Complete the working.

Find the cost of one toilet roll first, then compare prices.

6 toilet rolls costs \$4.02, so 1 costs \$4.02 ÷ 6 = ...

10 toilet rolls costs \$6.80, so 1 costs \$6.80 ÷ 10 = ...

The ...... pack is better value as it costs ...... cents less per toilet roll.

2 A 300 g bag of rice costs \$3.36. A 500 g bag of rice costs \$5.40.

Which bag is the better value for money?
Complete the working.

The masses of the bags are in multiples of 100 g, so find the cost of 100 g of each, then compare.

300 g costs \$3.36, so 100 g costs \$3.36 ÷ 3 = ...

500 g costs \$5.40, so 100 g costs \$5.40 ÷ 5 = ...

The ...... g bag is better value as it costs ......cents less per 100 g.

3 Sasha buys 5 packets of crisps for \$7.25.
How much do 3 packets cost?

Complete the working.

This is called the 'unitary method'. You find the cost of one packet, then use this answer to find the cost of three packets.

1 packet costs \$7.25 ÷ 5 = ...

3 packets cost ...... × 3 = ...

4 Shen buys 6 tins of beans for \$4.92. How much do 15 tins cost?

Complete the working.

1 tin costs \$4.92 ÷ 6 = ...

15 tins cost ...... × 15 = ...

Now try Exercise 14.2 on page 138 of Coursebook 9.

15 Area, perimeter and volume

15.1 Solving circle problems

You already know the formula for the circumference of a circle:

Circumference = $\pi \times$ diameter or $C = \pi \times d$

So far, the value you have used for π is 3.14.
This is not very accurate.

When you use the 'π' button on your calculator, you get a more accurate answer.

Press the 'π' button on your calculator and you will see that the value of the π button on your calculator is 3.141592654...

In all the question below, use the 'π' button on your calculator. Round your answers to 2 decimal places.

1 Complete the workings to find the circumference of these circles.

a

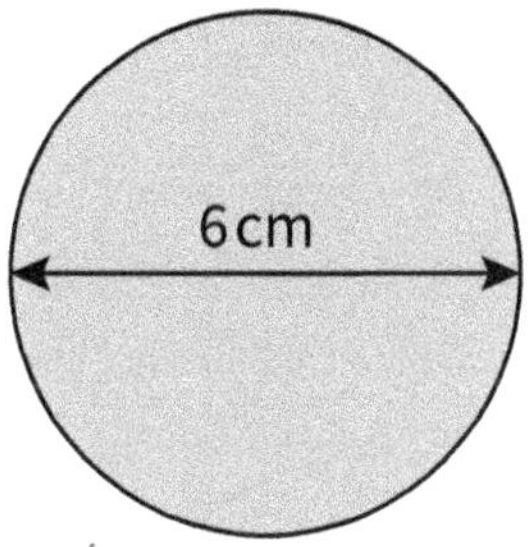

$d = 6$ cm

$C = \pi \times d = \pi \times 6$

= .... cm

b

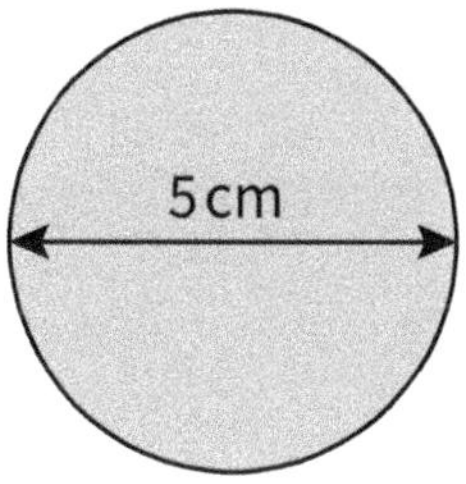

$d = 5$ cm

$C = \pi \times d = \pi \times$ ......

= .... cm

c

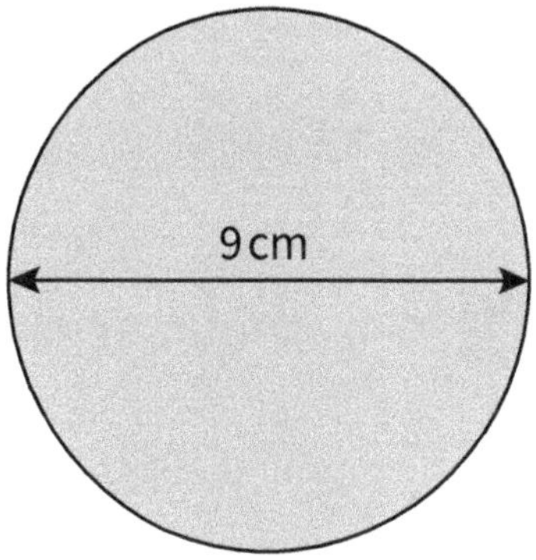

$d =$ ...... cm

$C = \pi \times d = \pi \times$ ......

= .... cm

2 Complete the working to find the circumference of this circle.

radius, $r = 4$ cm

diameter, $d = 2 \times 4 =$ .... cm

$C = \pi \times d = \pi \times$ .... = ... cm

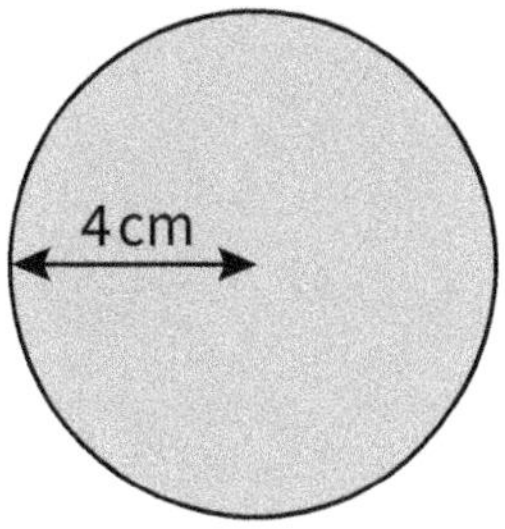

Remember that the diameter is twice the radius.

3 Complete the workings to find the perimeter of this semicircle.

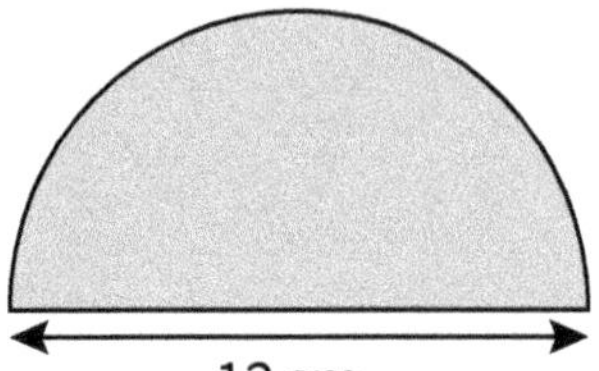

Perimeter of semicircle = diameter + circumference of the circle ÷ 2

Find the circumference of the circle first:

$C = \pi \times d = \pi \times 12 =$ .... cm

$\frac{1}{2}$ of the circumference = ... ÷ 2 = ... cm

Perimeter = 12 + ... = ... cm

The perimeter of the semicircle is the distance around the outside. This is the diameter plus half of the circumference of the circle.

Remember, the formula for the area of a circle is:

Area = $\pi \times$ radius^2 or $A = \pi \times r^2$

4 Complete the workings to find the area of these circles.

a

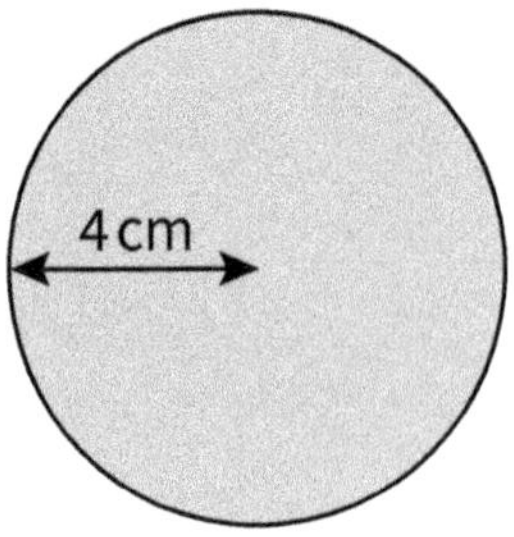

$r = 4$ cm

$A = \pi \times r^2 = \pi \times 4^2$

$= \pi \times 16$

= .... cm^2

b

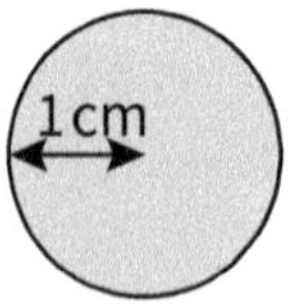

$r = 1$ cm

$A = \pi \times r^2 = \pi \times 1^2$

$= \pi \times$ ......

= .... cm^2

c

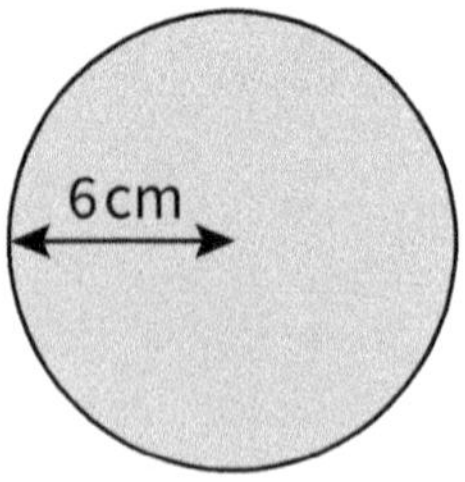

$r =$ ...... cm

$A = \pi \times r^2 = \pi \times$ ......^{2}

$= \pi \times$ ......

= .... cm^2

5 Complete the working to find the area of this circle.

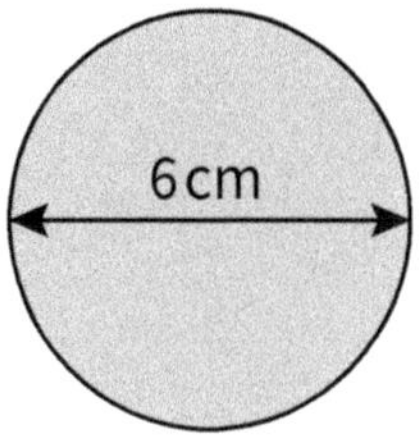

diameter, $d = 6$ cm   radius, $r = 6 \div 2 = \ldots\ldots$ cm

$A = \pi \times r^2 = \pi \times \ldots\ldots^2$

$= \pi \times \ldots\ldots = \ldots\ldots\ldots\ldots$ cm^2

6 Complete the workings to find the area of this semicircle.

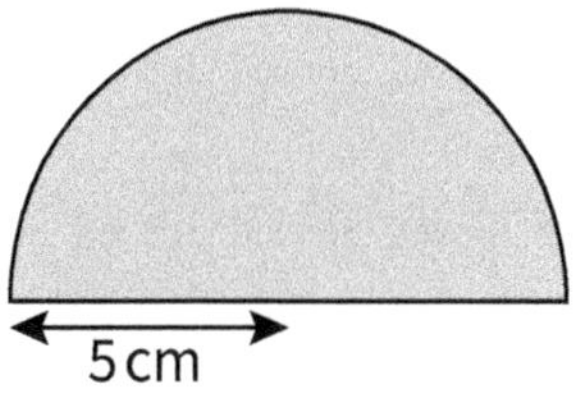

Area of semicircle = area of circle ÷ 2

Find the area of the circle first:

$A = \pi \times r^2 = \pi \times \ldots\ldots^2$

$= \pi \times \ldots\ldots = \ldots\ldots\ldots\ldots$ cm^2

Area of semicircle = ... ÷ 2 = ... cm^2

The area of a semicircle is half of the area of a circle.

7 Complete the workings to find the area of this semicircle.

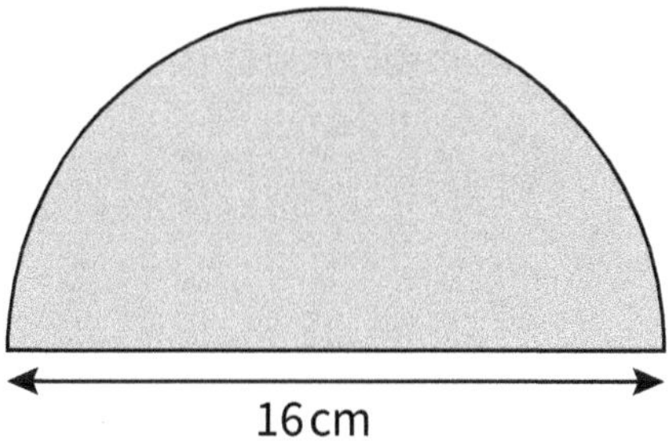

Radius = ... ÷ 2 = ... cm

Area of circle $= \pi \times r^2 = \pi \times \ldots\ldots^2$

$= \pi \times \ldots\ldots = \ldots\ldots\ldots\ldots$ cm^2

Area of semicircle = ... ÷ 2 = ... cm^2

Now try Exercise 15.3 on page 146 of Coursebook 9.

15.2 Calculating with prisms and cylinders

A prism is a 3D shape that has the same **cross-section** along its length.

This shape is a prism. It is called a triangular prism.

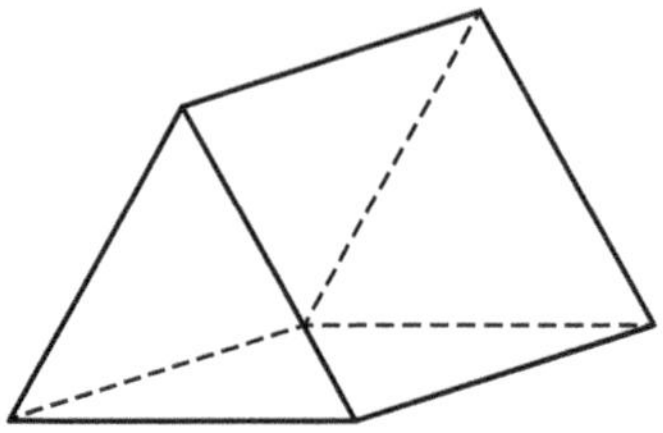

The triangle is the shape of the cross-section.

It has the shape of the same triangle along its whole length.

This shape is NOT a prism. It has four triangular faces. It is called a triangular-based pyramid or tetrahedron.

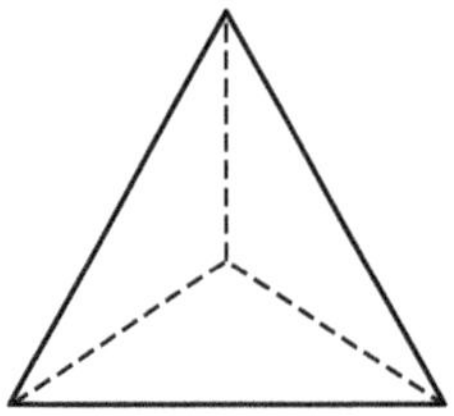

1 Next to each of these shapes put a tick (✓) if it is a prism. Put a cross (✗) if it is not a prism.

a

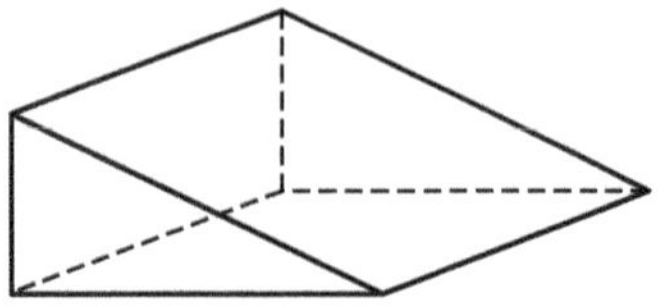

b

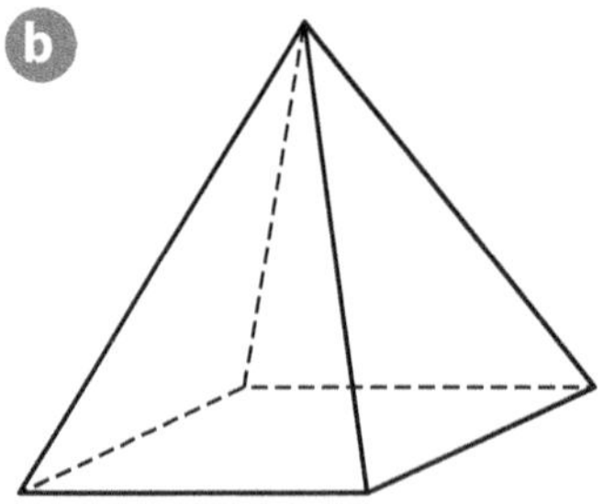

c

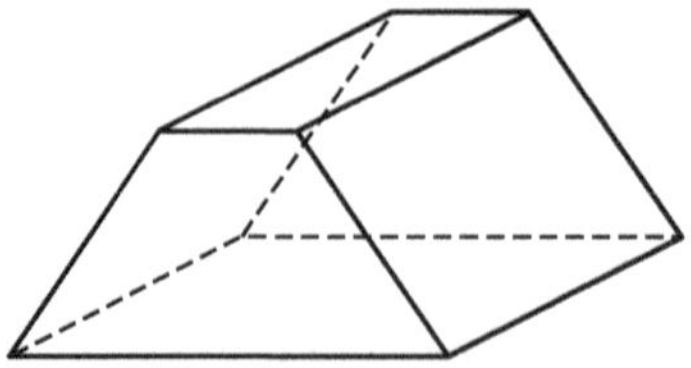

d

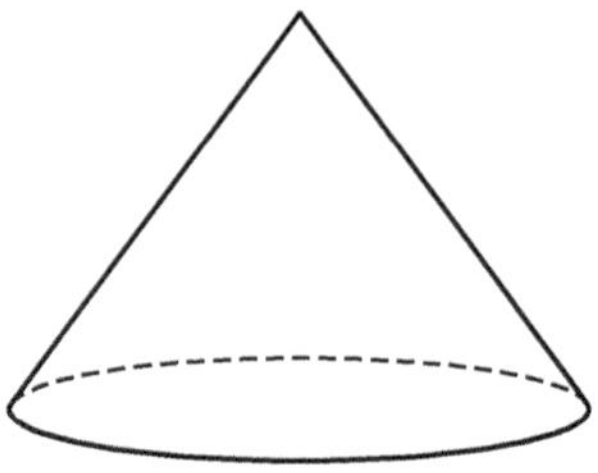

e

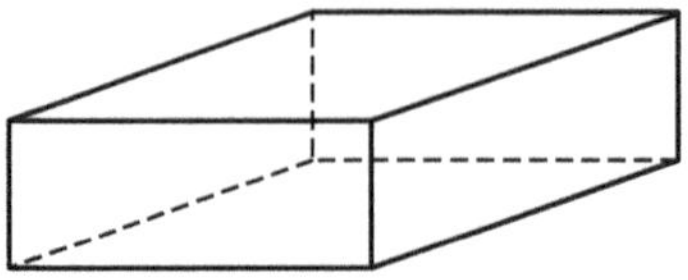

f

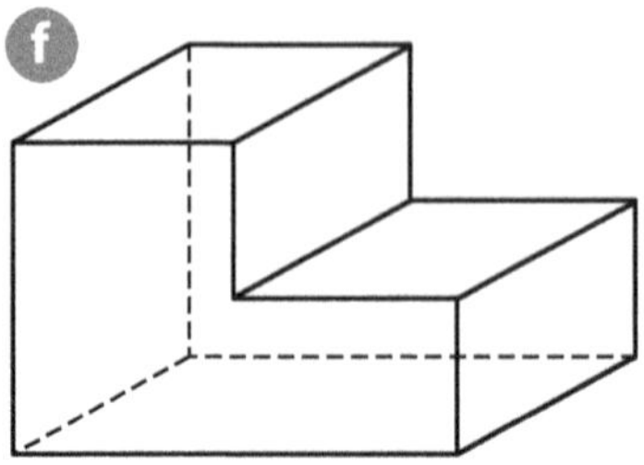

You work out the volume of a prism using the formula:

Volume = area of cross-section × length

2 Complete the workings to find the volume of each prism.

a

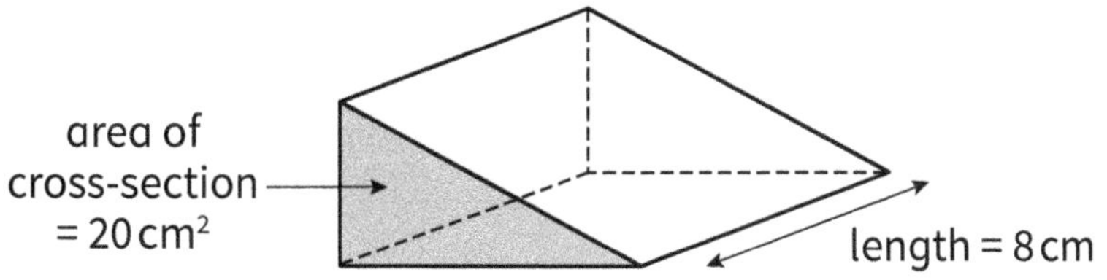

Volume = area of cross-section × length

$= 20 \times 8 = \ldots\ldots \text{ cm}^3$

b

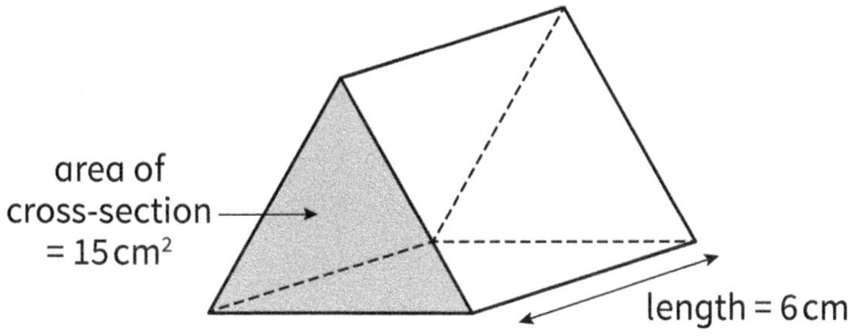

Volume = area of cross-section × length

$= \ldots\ldots \times \ldots\ldots = \ldots\ldots \text{ cm}^3$

c

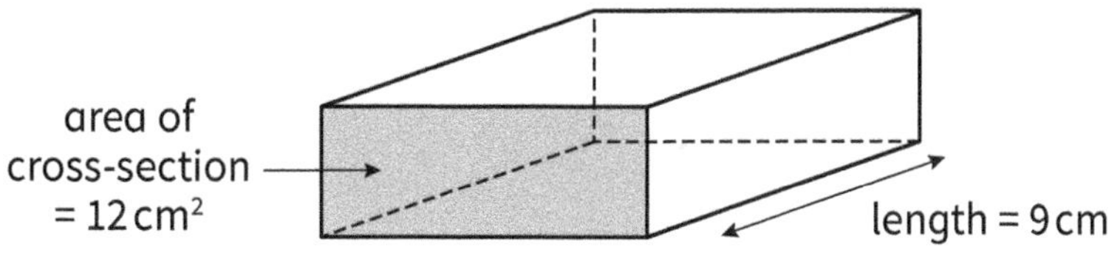

Volume = area of cross-section × length

$= \ldots\ldots \times \ldots\ldots = \ldots\ldots \text{ cm}^3$

d

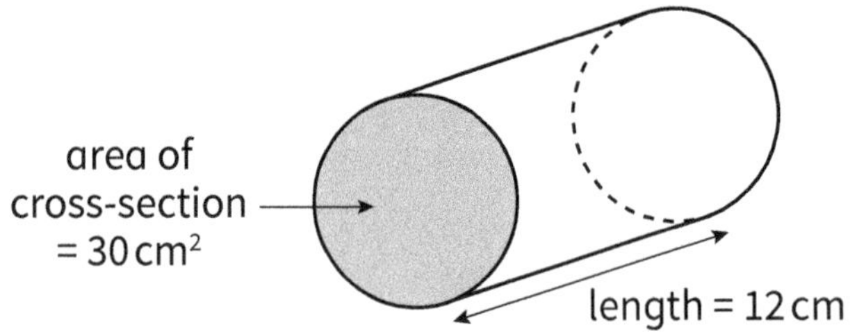

Volume = area of cross-section × length

= ...... × ...... = ... cm^3

3 Complete the workings to find the volume of each prism.

In these prisms, you need to work out the area of the cross-section first, then work out the volume.

a

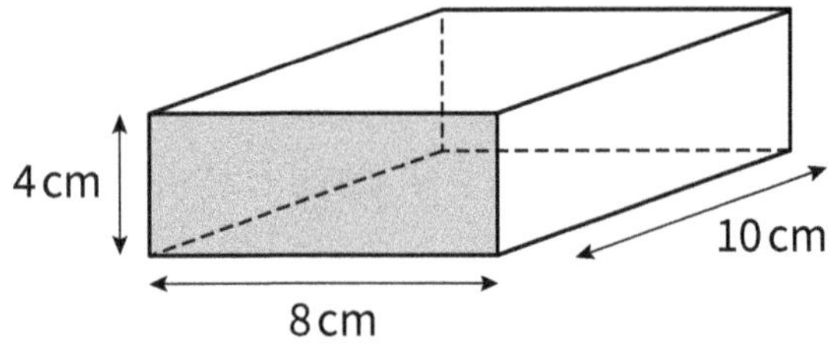

Area of cross-section = area of rectangle

= base × height = 8 × 4 = ... cm^2

Volume = area of cross-section × length

= ...... × 10 = ... cm^3

b

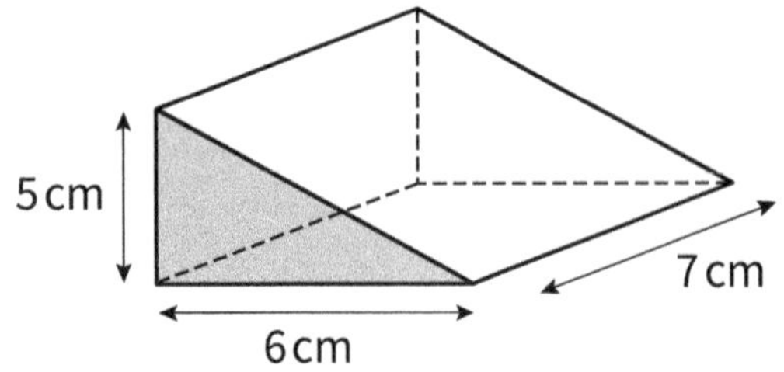

Area of cross-section = area of triangle

$= \frac{1}{2} \times$ base × height $= \frac{1}{2} \times 6 \times 5 =$ ...... cm^2

Volume = area of cross-section × length

= ...... × 7 = ... cm^3

c

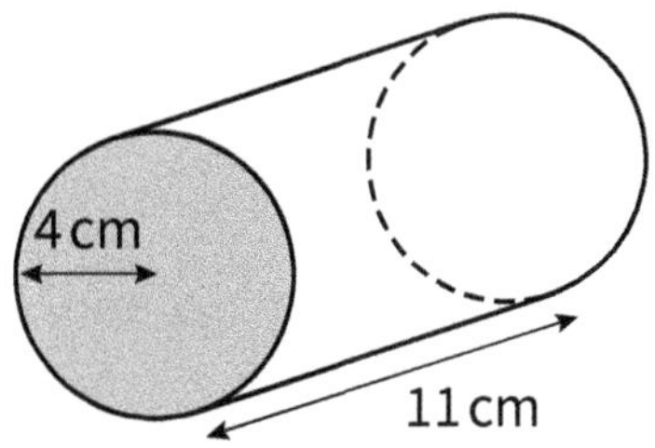

Use the 'π' button on your calculator. Round your answer to 2 decimal places.

Area of cross-section = area of circle

$= \pi \times r^2 = \pi \times ......^2$

$= \pi \times ......$ = ... cm^2

Volume = area of cross-section × length

= .... × 11 = ... cm^3

Now try Exercise 15.4 on page 148 of Coursebook 9.

16 Probability

16.1 Calculating probabilities

A probability is a number between 0 and 1. You can write it as a fraction, a decimal or a percentage.

There are seven days in a week. The probability that a birthday is on a Saturday or a Sunday this year is $\frac{2}{7}$ or 0.29 to 2 d.p. On a calculator $2 \div 7 = 0.285714\ldots$ or 29% (0.29 = 29%).

1 Write these probabilities as decimals and percentages.

Fraction	$\frac{2}{7}$	$\frac{3}{5}$	$\frac{9}{10}$	$\frac{2}{3}$	$\frac{3}{11}$	$\frac{7}{15}$
Decimal (2 d.p.)	0.29					
Percentage	29%					

2 Here ten cards.

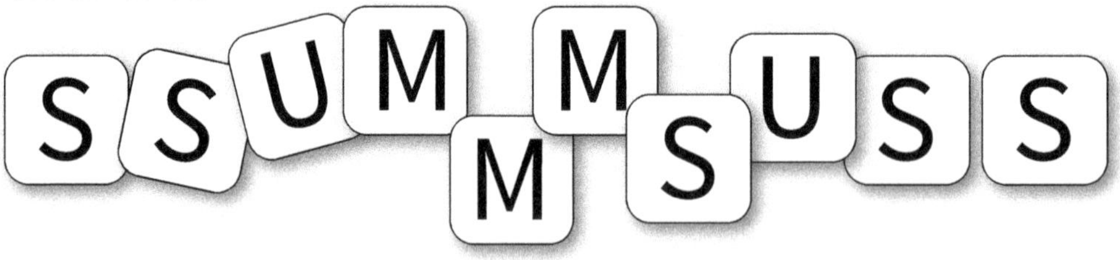

One card is chosen at random.

a Find the probability that it is:

i S...... **ii** U...... **iii** M......

b Show that the three probabilities add up to 1.

....

3 In a class there are 7 boys and 13 girls. A student is chosen at random.

a Find the probability the student is:

i a boy ...... **ii** a girl ......

b Show that the two probabilities add up to 1.

....

The probability that it will rain today is 65%.

The probability it will NOT rain is 100% – 65% = 35%.

This is because the probabilities must add up to 100%.

4 **a** The probability the sun will shine today is 10%.

The probability the sun will NOT shine today is ......

b The probability the sun will shine tomorrow is 45%.

The probability the sun will NOT shine tomorrow is ......

5 **a** The probability Anders will pass his driving test is 0.8.

The probability Anders will fail his driving test is ......

b The probability Sasha will pass his driving test is 0.95.

The probability Sasha will fail his driving test is ......

6 A plane can land early, on time or late. Fill in the missing probability.

Arrive	early	on time	late
Probability	10%	65%	

7 Jasmine takes a music examination. Four grades are possible: Fail, Pass, Merit or Distinction. Fill in the missing probability.

Grade	Fail	Pass	Merit	Distinction
Probability		45%	30%	10%

8 There are four colours on a spinner. Each has a different probability. Fill in the missing probability.

Colour	red	green	blue	yellow
Probability	0.13	0.46		0.22

Now try Exercise 16.1 on page 152 of Coursebook 9.

16.2 Sample space diagrams

Here are two spinners.

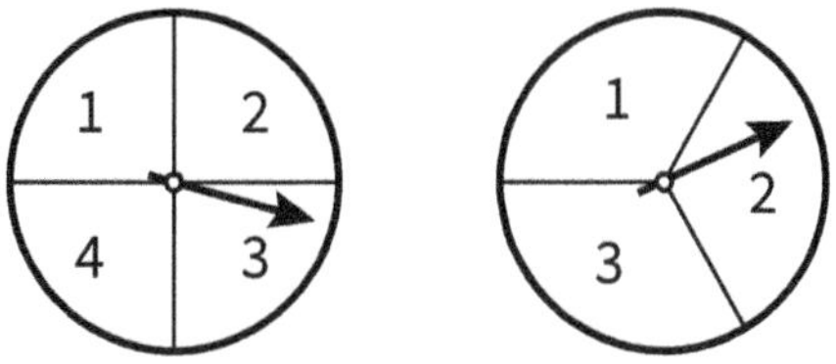

One has four equal sections. The other has three equal sections.

You can show all the possible outcomes on a **sample space diagram**.

Each cross is an outcome. There 12 outcomes.

The outcomes with a total of 5 are marked.

The probability of a total of 5 is $\frac{3}{12} = \frac{1}{4}$.

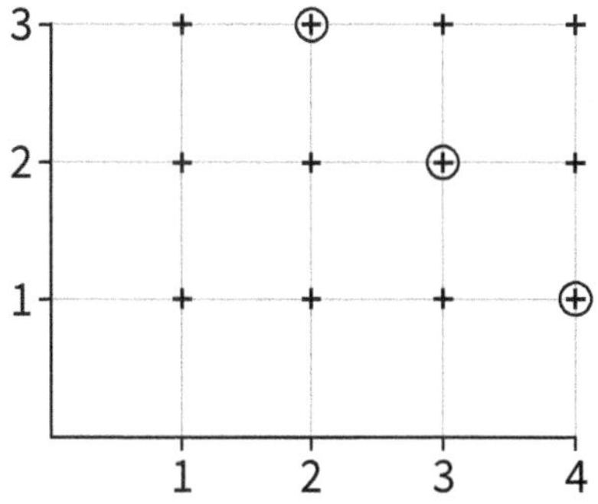

1 For the two spinners above, find the probability of:

a a total of 6 ...... **b** a total of 4 ......

c a total of 7 ...... **d** a total of 2 ......

2 Here are two spinners.

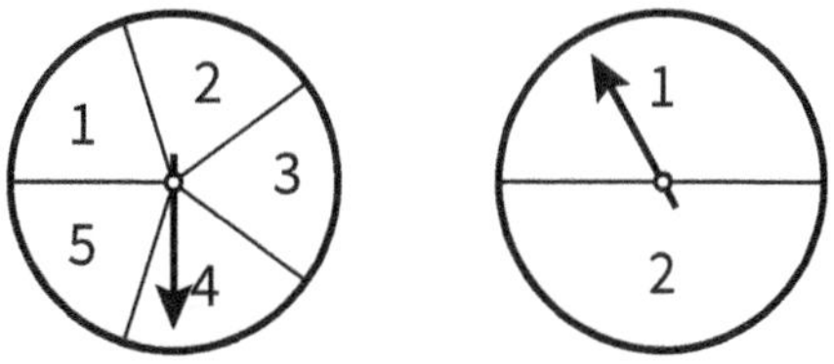

a Draw a sample space diagram for these spinners.

b What is the largest possible total? ......

c Find the probability of a total of:

i 6...... **ii** 4...... **iii** 2......

3 Here are two spinners.

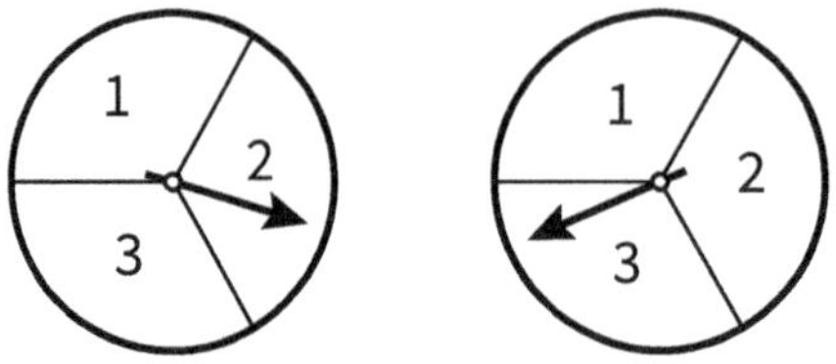

a Draw a sample space diagram for these spinners.

b What is the largest possible total? ......

c Find the probability of a total of:

i 5...... **ii** 4...... **iii** 3......

4 Here are two spinners.

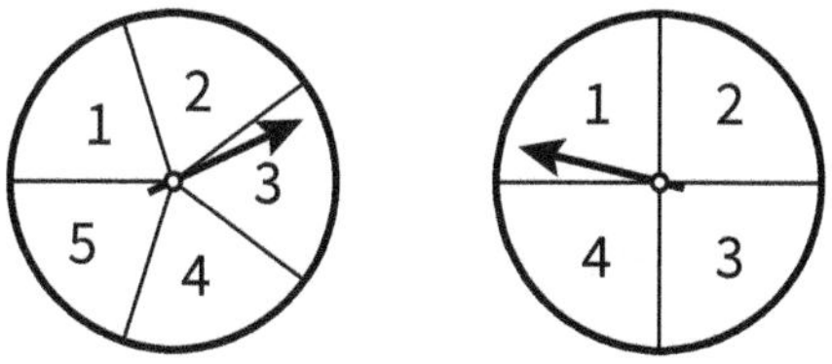

a Draw a sample space diagram for these spinners.

b Find the probability of a total of:

i 8...... **ii** 6...... **iii** 4......

Now try Exercise 16.2 on page 154 of Coursebook 9.

17 Bearings and scale drawings

17.1 Using bearings

A **bearing** is an angle measured from north in a clockwise direction. It gives the direction of one object from another.

A bearing can have any value from 0° to 360°. It is always written with three figures.

Look at this diagram.

Imagine you must walk from **A** to **B**.

At A you must face north, then turn in a clockwise direction to face B.

You have turned through an angle of 70°.

So to get from **A** to **B** you would walk on a bearing of 070°.

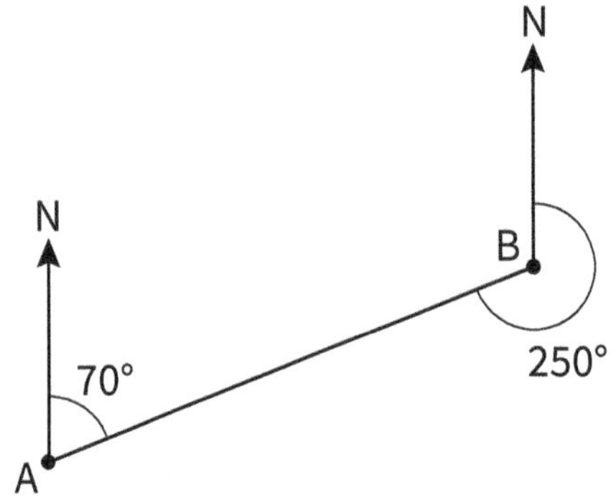

Imagine you must walk from **B** to **A**.

At B you must face north, then turn in a clockwise direction to face A.

You have turned through an angle of 250°.

So to get from **B** to **A** you would walk on a bearing of 250°.

1 Draw a line linking each diagram to the bearing you would need to walk on to get from A to B.

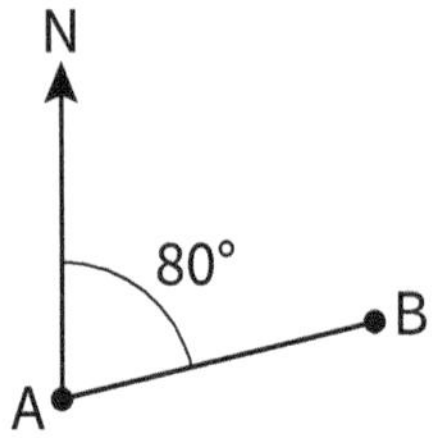

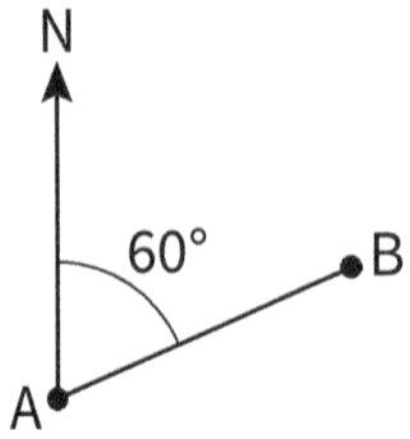

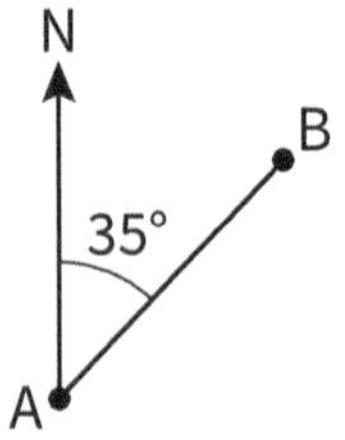

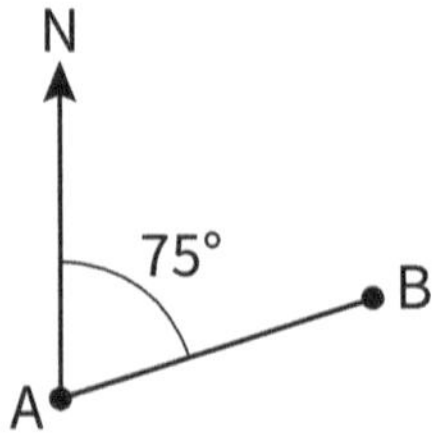

060°   075°   080°   035°

2 For each of these diagrams write down the bearing you would need to walk on to get from C to D.

a

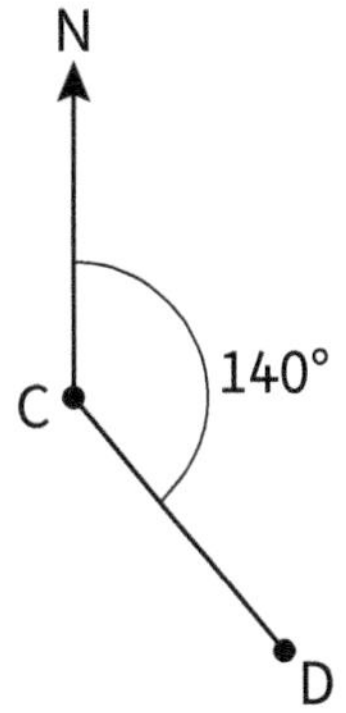

Bearing ......

b

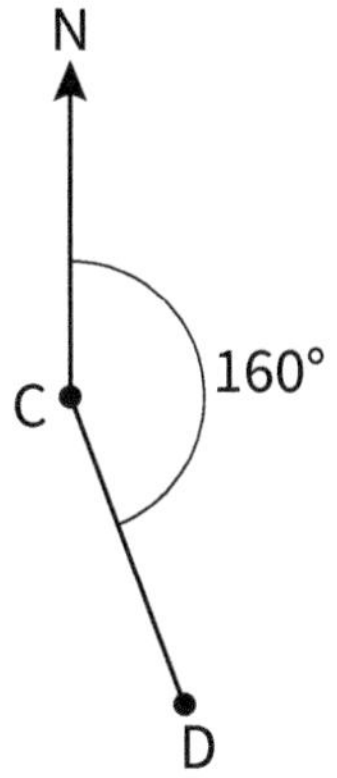

Bearing ......

c

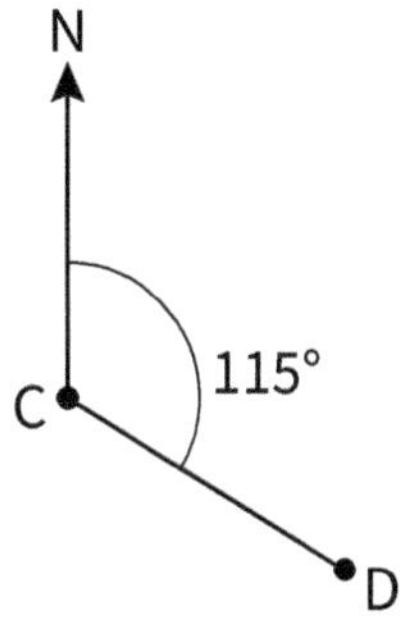

Bearing ......

d

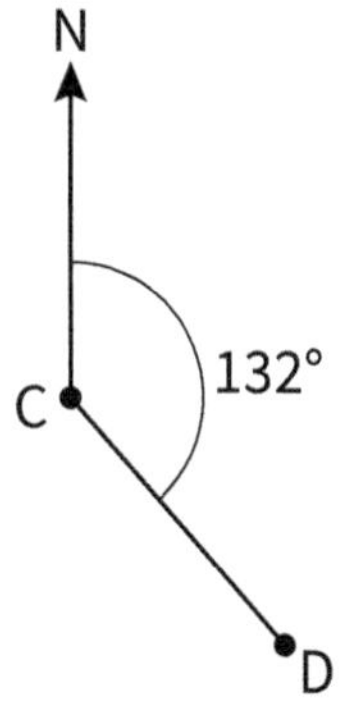

Bearing ......

3 Draw a line linking each diagram to the bearing you would need to walk on to get from A to B.

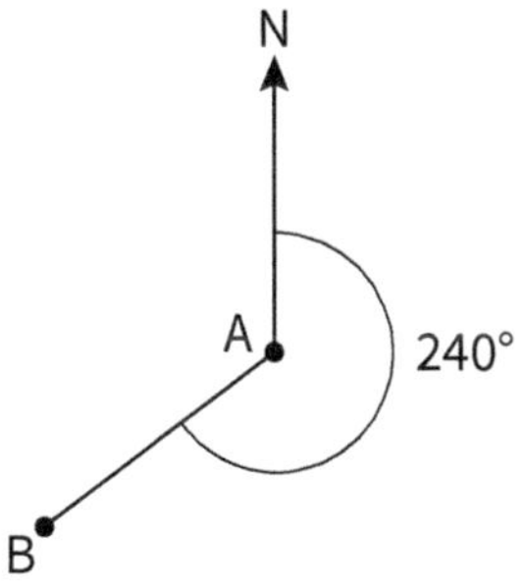

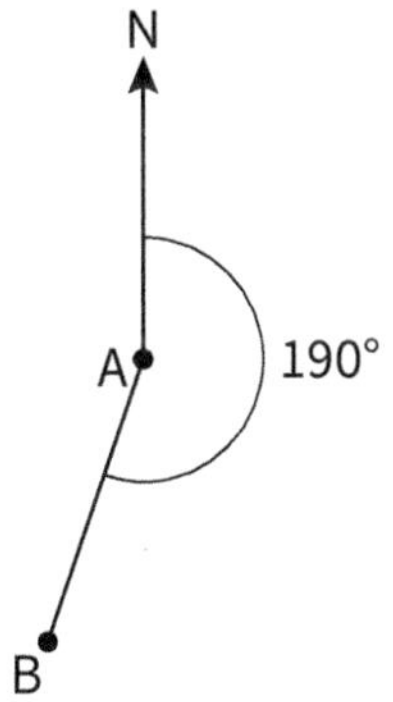

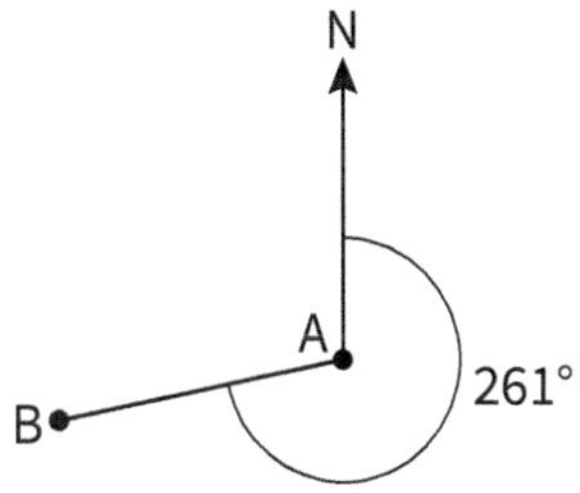

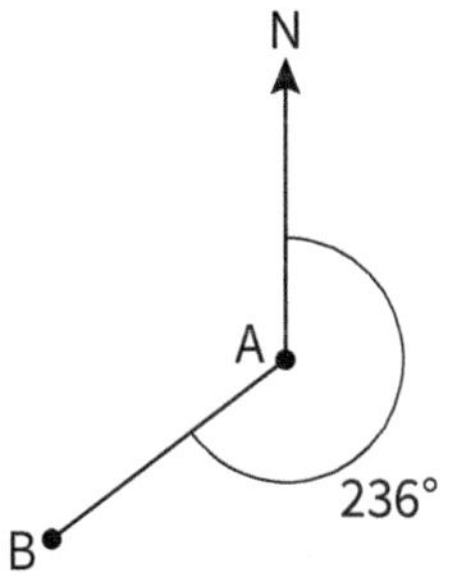

190°

236°

240°

261°

4 For each of these diagrams write down the bearing you would need to walk on to get from C to D.

a

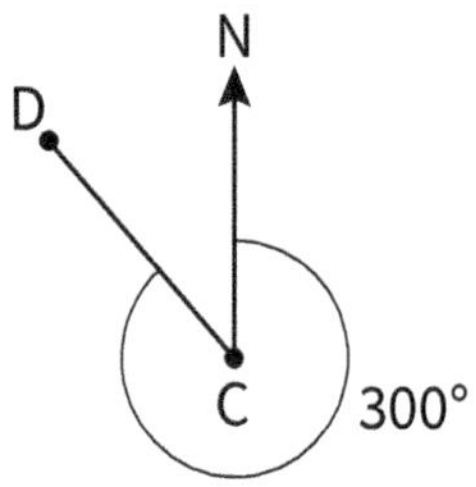

Bearing ......

b

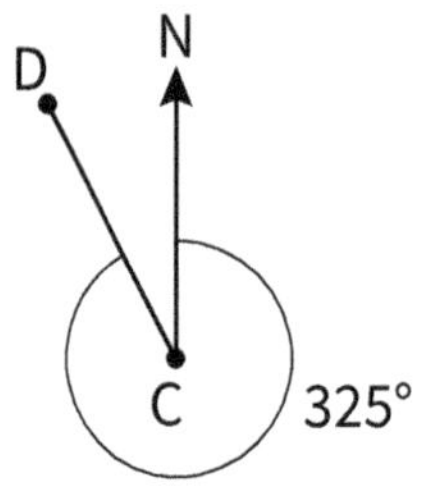

Bearing ......

c

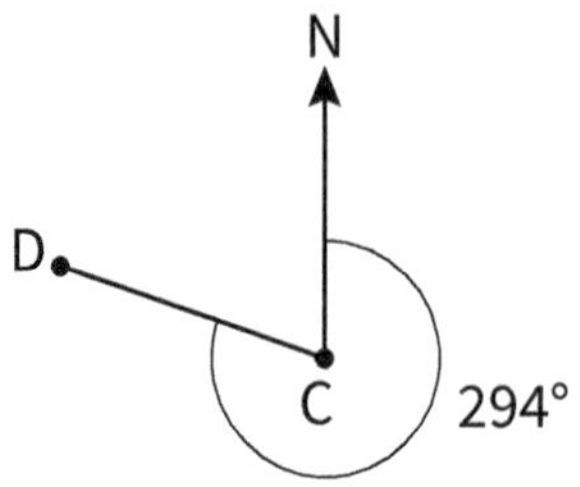

Bearing ......

d

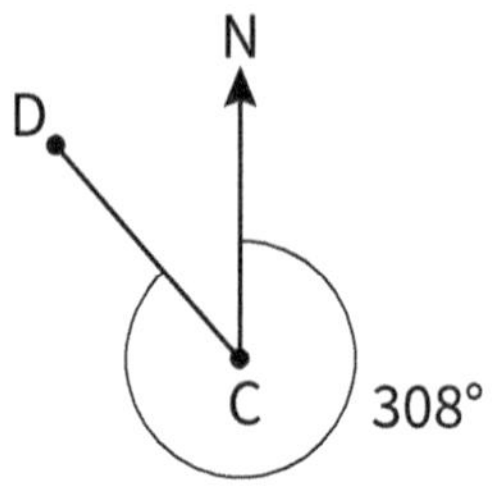

Bearing ......

5 Use a protractor to measure each of the angles shown.

Write down the bearing you would need to walk on to get from X to Y.

a

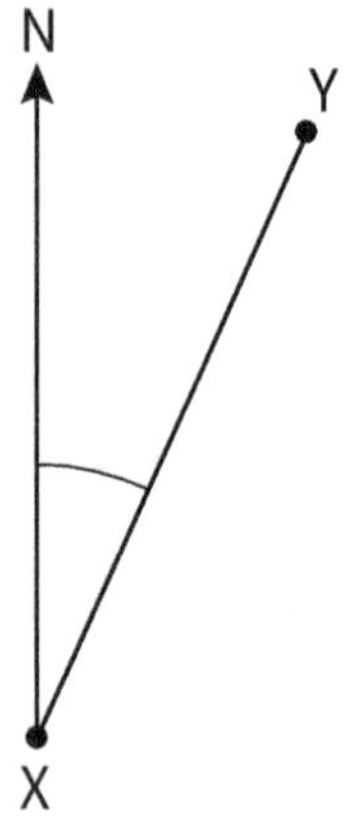

Bearing ......

b

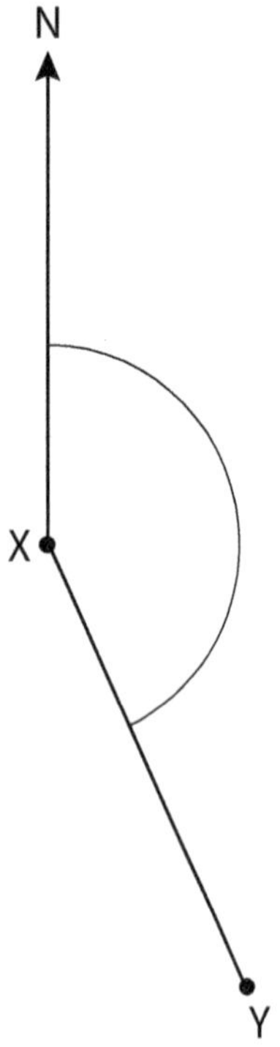

Bearing ......

c

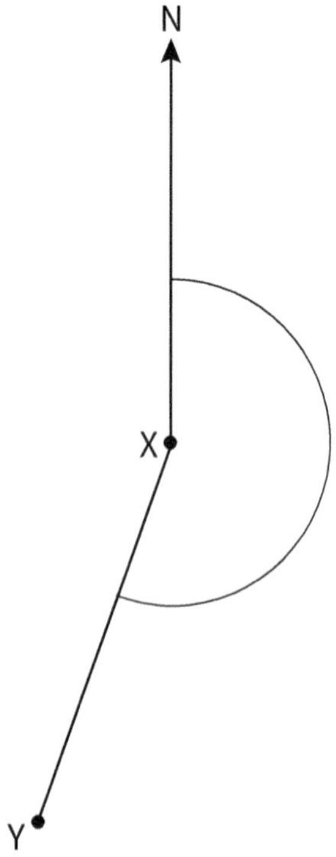

Bearing ......

Now try Exercise 17.1 on page 159 of Coursebook 9.

17.2 Making scale drawings

When making a scale drawing, always measure the lengths and angles accurately.

You will need to use the scale to convert distances on the ground to distances on the map.

Look at the following example:

A map has a scale of 1 cm represents 2 km.

How far on the ground is 3 cm on the map?

3 cm on the map would measure $3 \times 2 = 6$ km on the ground.

> Map to ground:
> MULTIPLY by scale.

How far on the map is 10 km on the ground?

10 km on the ground would measure $10 \div 2 = 5$ cm on the map.

> Ground to map:
> DIVIDE by scale.

1 A map has a scale of 1 cm represents 5 km. Draw lines linking each grey map distance with its correct white ground distance. The first one has been done for you.

Map distance	Ground distance
2 cm	60 km
8 cm	100 km
12 cm	10 km
9 cm	25 km
20 cm	45 km
5 cm	40 km

2 A map has a scale of 1 cm represents 12 km.

a How far on the ground are these distances on the map?

i 2 cm ....

ii 5 cm ....

iii 10 cm ....

b How far on the map are these distances on the ground?

i 36 km ....

ii 48 km ....

iii 96 km ....

3 A map has a scale of 1 cm represents 8 km.

a How far on the ground is 4.5 cm on the map? $4.5 \times 8 =$ ...... km

b How far on the map is 18 km on the ground? $18 \div 8 =$ ...... cm

4 Follow the steps to draw a scale drawing for each of these journeys.

Use a scale of 1 cm represents 10 km.

a A ship leaves harbour and sails 60 km on a bearing of 120°.

Step 1: Put the centre of your protractor on the dot for the harbour, and line up 0° with the north arrow. Make a mark at 120°.

Step 2: Work out the distance the ship sails using the scale. 60 km ÷ 10 = ... cm

Step 3: Join the dot for the harbour with your mark for 120° with a straight line that is exactly 6 cm long.

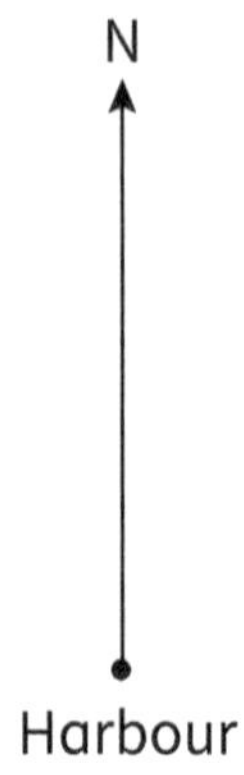

b A ship leaves an island and sails 85 km on a bearing of 035°.

Step 1: Put the centre of your protractor on the dot for the island, and line up 0° with the north arrow. Make a mark at 35°.

Step 2: Work out the distance the ship sails using the scale. 85 km ÷ 10 = ... cm

Step 3: Join the dot for the harbour with your mark for 35° with a straight line that is exactly ...... cm long.

5 Maha leaves her house and walks on a footpath for 8 km on a bearing of 095°.

Draw a scale drawing of her journey using a scale of 1 cm represents 2 km.

Now try Exercise 17.2 on page 162 of Coursebook 9.

18.1 Gradient of a graph

The **gradient** measures the steepness of this line.

Use the triangle.

$$\text{Gradient} = \frac{\text{height}}{\text{width}} = \frac{3}{5}$$

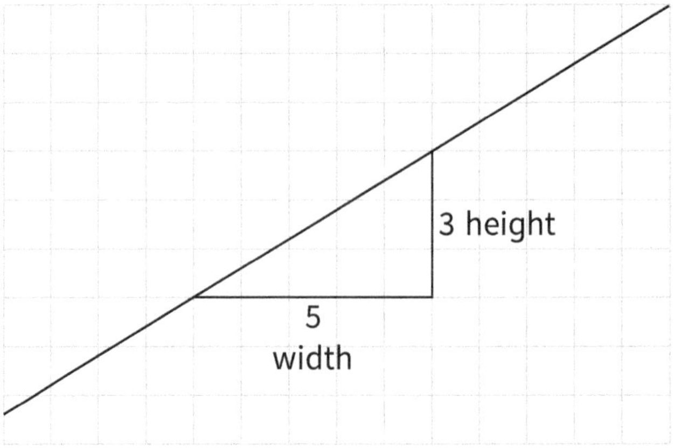

1 Find the gradients of these lines.

a

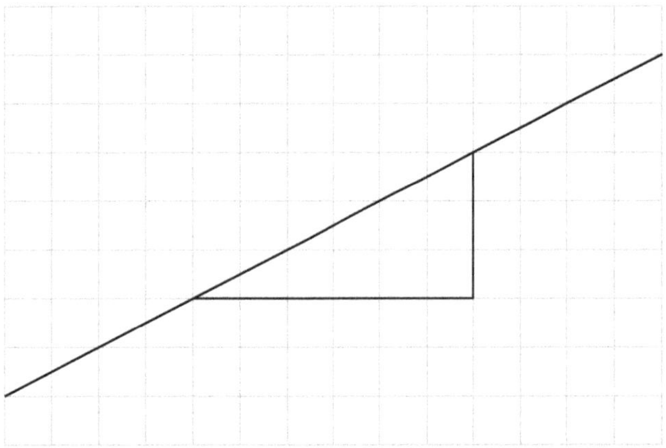

Gradient = ……

b

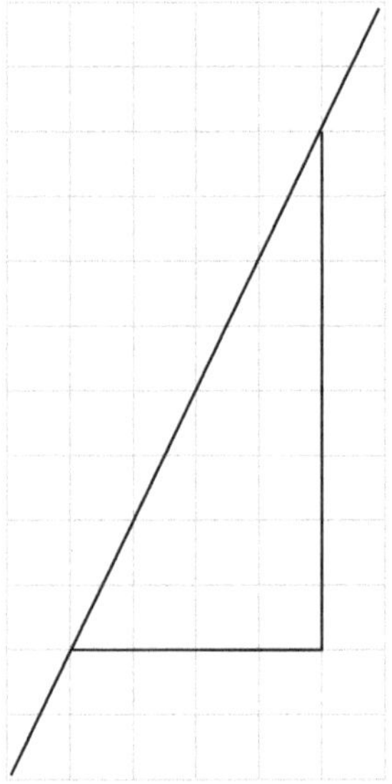

Gradient = ……

c

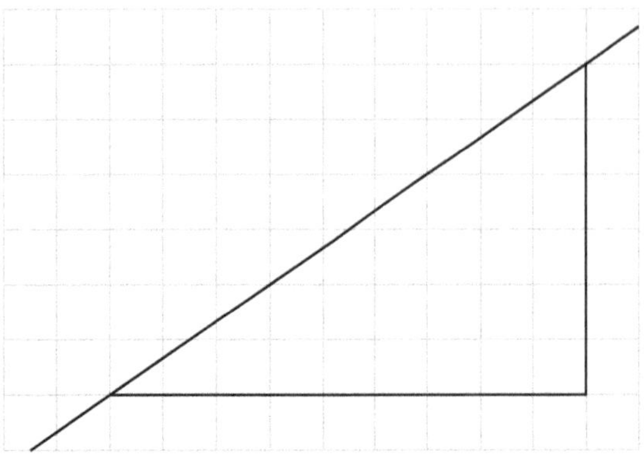

Gradient = ……

d

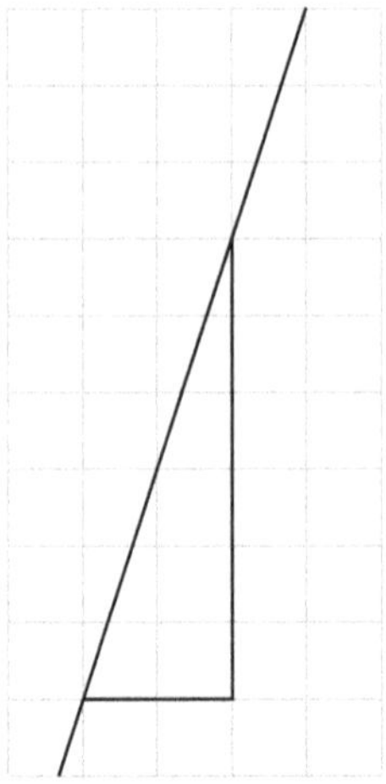

Gradient = ……

e

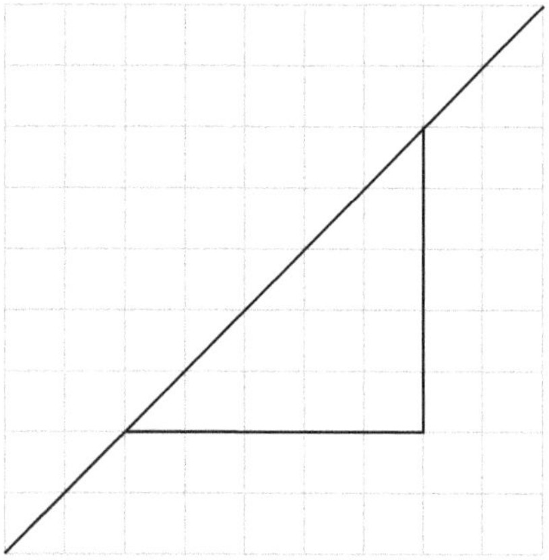

If a line slopes down from left to right, it has a negative gradient.

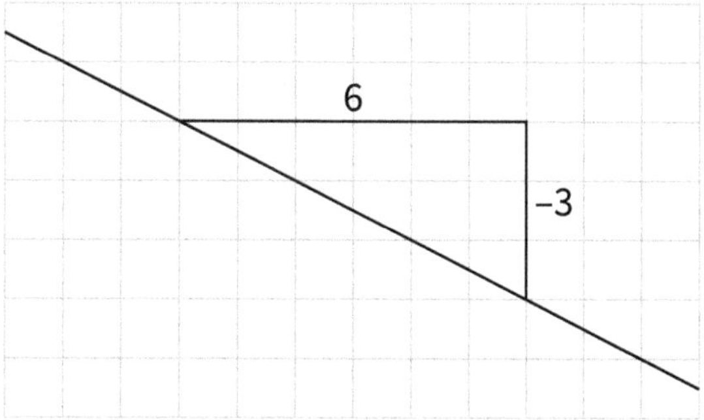

The gradient of this line is $\frac{-3}{6} = \frac{-1}{2}$

2 Find the gradients of these lines.

a

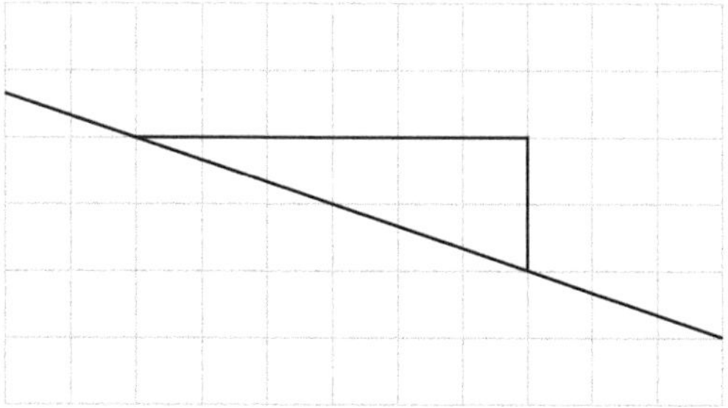

Gradient = ...

b

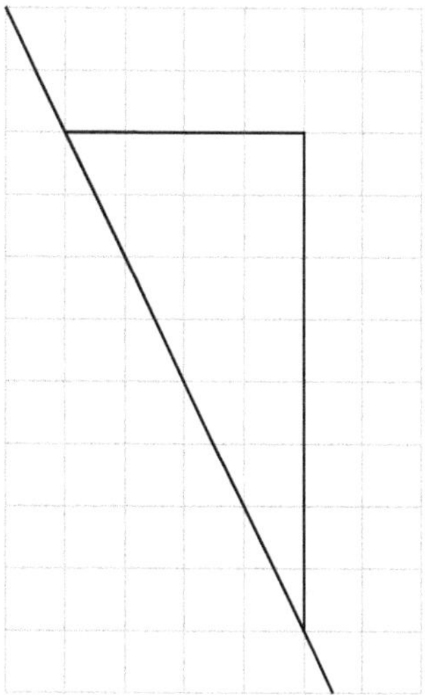

Gradient = ...

c

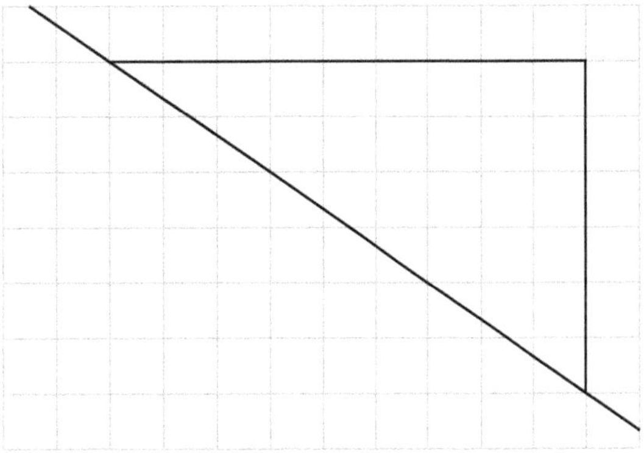

Gradient = ...

d

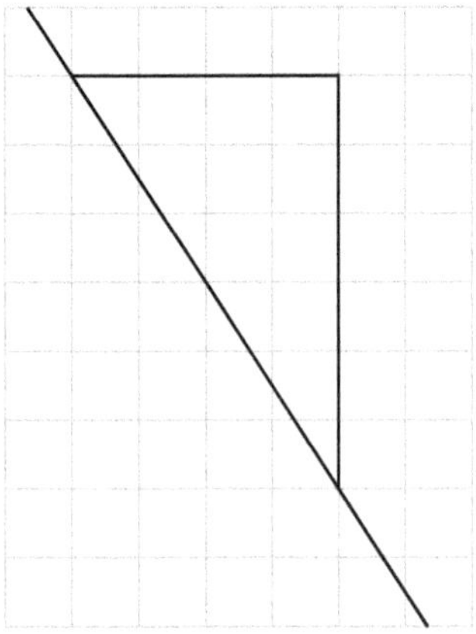

Gradient = ...

3

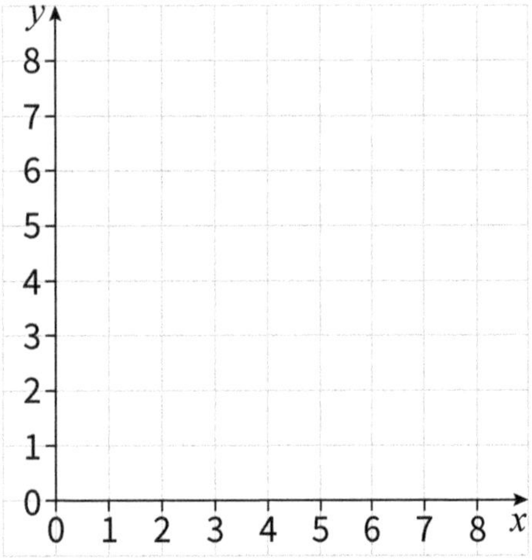

a On this grid, plot the points (2, 2) and (8, 5) and join them up.

b Find the gradient of the line. ......

4

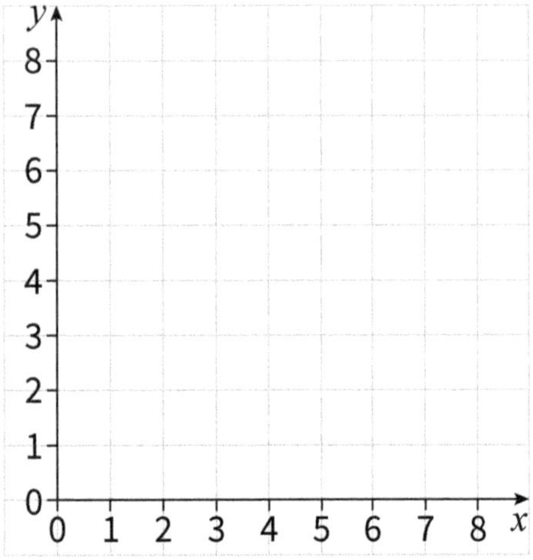

a On this grid, plot the points (3, 7) and (6, 1) and join them up.

b Find the gradient of the line ......

5

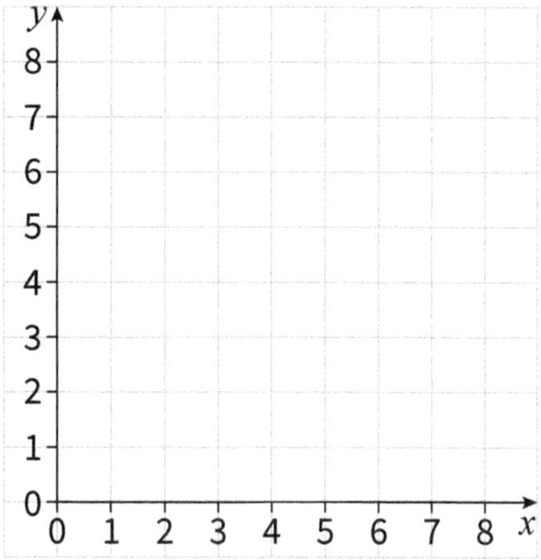

a On this grid, plot the points (3, 0) and (5, 8) and join them up.

b Find the gradient of the line. ......

6

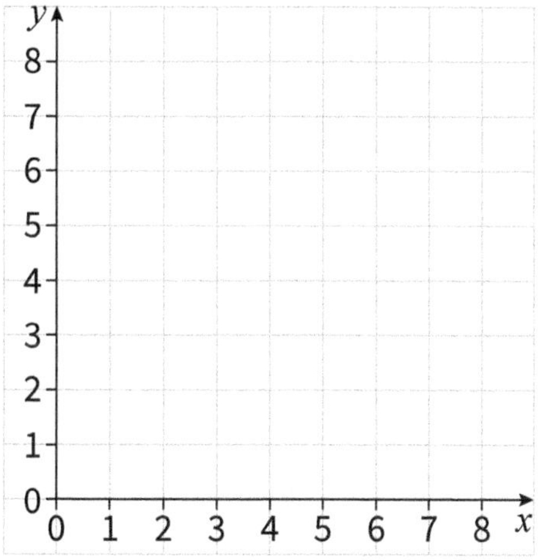

a On this grid, plot the points (1, 6) and (7, 4) and join them up.

b Find the gradient of the line ......

Now try Exercise 18.1 on page 166 of Coursebook 9.

18.2 The graph of $y = mx + c$

If m and c are numbers, then the graph of $y = mx + c$ is a straight line.

1 **a** Complete this table.

x	0	1	2	4	5
$y = x + 3$	3		5		

b You have the coordinates of five points.

Plot them on this grid and join them with a straight line.

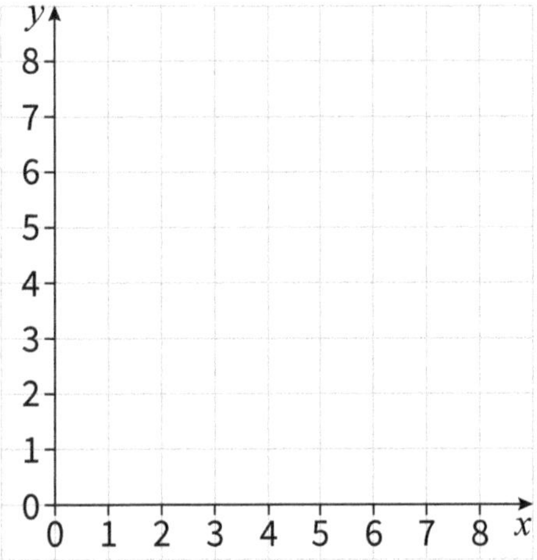

c Label your line with the equation $y = x + 3$.

d Find the gradient of the line ......

e Complete this table.

x	2	3	5	7	8
$y = x - 2$	0		3		

f Plot the points from this table on the grid above. Join them with a straight line. Label the line with the equation $y = x - 2$.

g Find the gradient of this second line.

....

2 **a** Complete this table.

x	0	1	2	3	4
$y = 2x$		2		6	

b Plot the points on this grid and join them with a straight line.

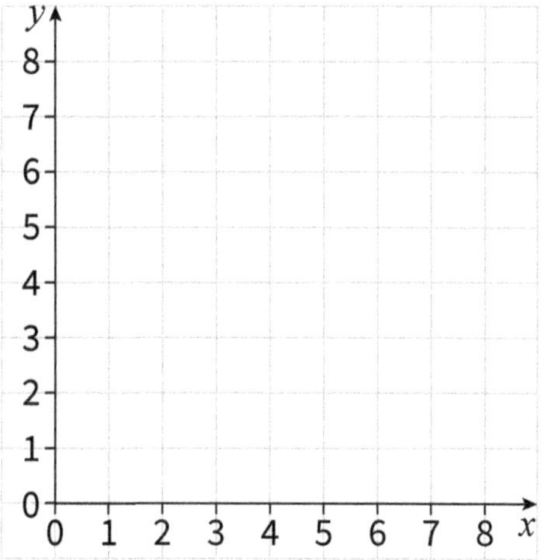

c Label your line with the equation $y = 2x$.

d Find the gradient of the line. ......

e Complete this table.

x	3	4	5	6
$y = 2x - 5$	1		5	

f Plot the points from this table on the grid above. Join them with a straight line. Label the line with the equation $y = 2x - 5$.

g Find the gradient of this second line. ......

3 **a** Complete this table.

x	0	2	4	6	8
$y = \frac{1}{2}x$				3	

b Plot the points on this grid and join them with a straight line.

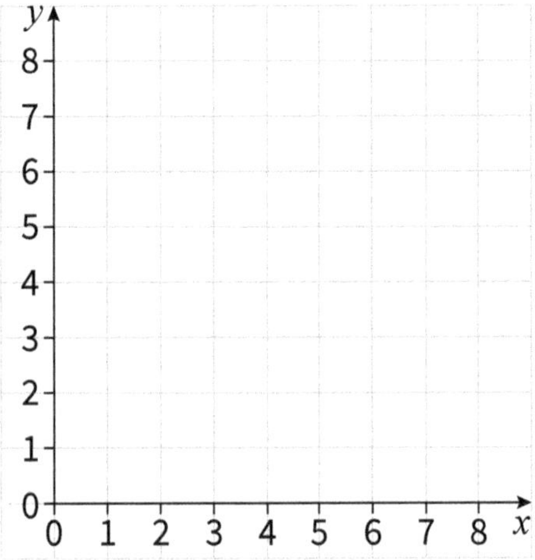

c Label your line with the equation $y = \frac{1}{2}x$.

d Find the gradient of the line. ……

e Complete this table.

x	0	2	4	6	8
$y = \frac{1}{2}x + 4$		5			

f Plot the points from this table on the grid above. Join them with a straight line. Label the line with the equation $y = \frac{1}{2}x + 4$

g Find the gradient of this second line. ……

Now try Exercise 18.2 on page 168 of Coursebook 9.

19 Interpreting and discussing results

19.1 Interpreting and drawing frequency diagrams

When you draw a **frequency polygon** you plot the frequency against the **midpoint** of the class interval. You then join the points you have plotted with straight lines.

1 The table shows the time it takes for 45 students to complete a puzzle.

Time, t (seconds)	Frequency	Midpoint
$0 < t \leqslant 10$	1	5
$10 < t \leqslant 20$	6	15
$20 < t \leqslant 30$	8	25
$30 < t \leqslant 40$	11	
$40 < t \leqslant 50$	14	
$50 < t \leqslant 60$	5	

The midpoint is the number that is half way between the lower and upper values of the class.

Half way between 0 and 10 is 5.

a Complete the midpoint column in the table.

b Complete the frequency polygon for this data.

The first point is plotted at midpoint 5 and frequency 1, the second point is plotted at midpoint 15 and frequency 6, etc.

Time taken for students to complete puzzle

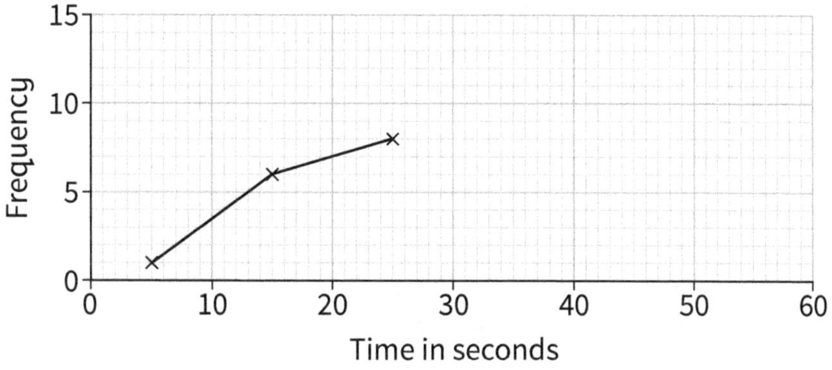

Now try Exercise 19.1 on page 179 of Coursebook 9.

19.2 Interpreting and drawing line graphs

A **line graph** shows you how data changes over a period of time.

You draw a line graph by plotting the points you are given. You then join the points using straight lines.

1 The table shows the average monthly temperature (°C) in Rio de Janeiro, Brazil.

Month	Jan	Feb	Mar	Apr	May	Jun	Jul	Aug	Sep	Oct	Nov	Dec
Temperature (°C)	26	27	26	25	23	22	21	22	22	23	24	25

a Complete the line graph below. The first three points have been plotted for you.

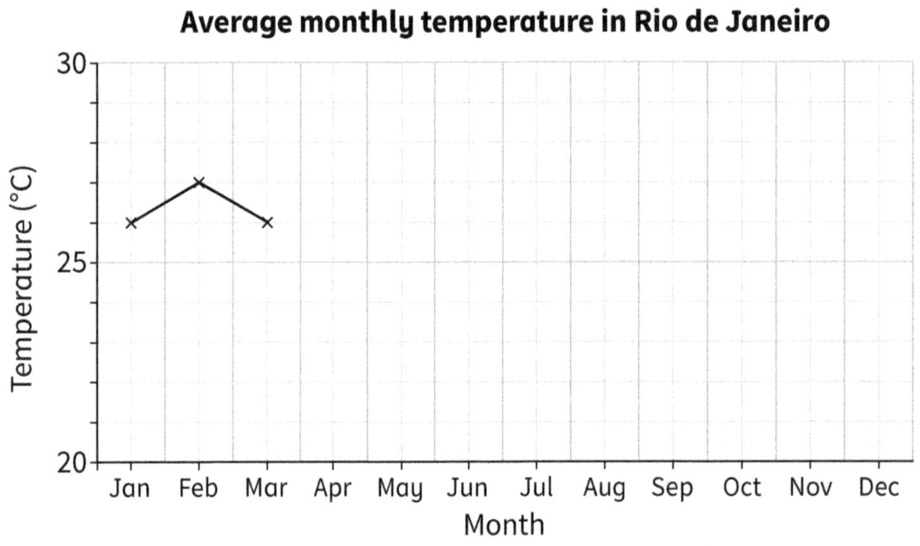

b Use your line graph to answer these questions:

i Which month has the highest average temperature? ....

ii Which month has the lowest average temperature? ....

iii Which of these statements correctly describes the trend in the data? ......

A At the start of the year the temperature in Rio de Janeiro is just over 25°C. It then gets warmer in the months of May, June and July and then starts to get colder again from August onwards.

B At the start of the year the temperature in Rio de Janeiro is just over 25°C. It then gets colder in the months of May, June and July and then starts to get warmer again from August onwards.

2 The table shows the average number of days it rains per month in Rio de Janeiro.

Month	Jan	Feb	Mar	Apr	May	Jun	Jul	Aug	Sep	Oct	Nov	Dec
Number of days it rains	13	11	12	10	10	7	7	7	11	13	13	14

a Complete the line graph below. The first three points have been plotted for you.

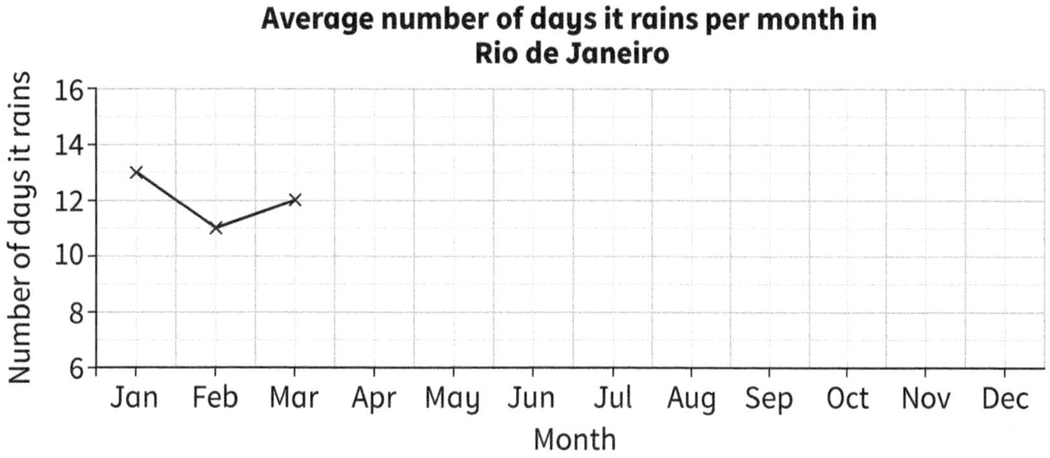

b **i** Which month has the most days of rain on average? ....

ii Describe the trend in the data ....

....

....

....

3 The table shows the number of tourists visiting Rio de Janeiro each year from 2009 to 2015.

Year	2009	2010	2011	2012	2013	2014	2015
Number of tourists (millions)	4.8	5.2	5.4	5.7	5.7	5.9	5.8

a Complete the line graph below. The first two points have been plotted for you.

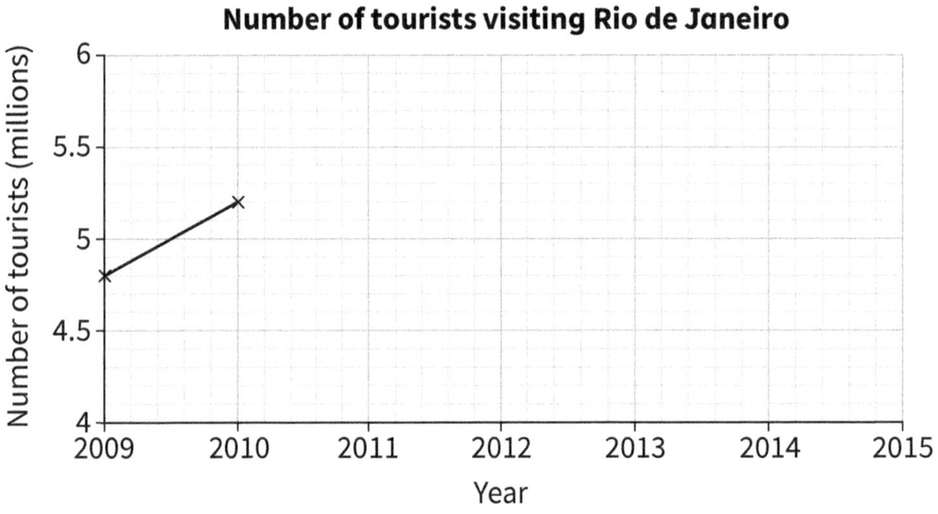

b Describe the trend in the data ....

....

....

....

Now try Exercise 19.2 on page 180 of Coursebook 9.

19.3 Interpreting and drawing scatter graphs

A **scatter graph** is a way of comparing two sets of data.

1 The table shows the French and Spanish test results of 15 students. Each test was marked out of 20.

French result	3	11	18	19	5	20	14	8	9	7	5	16	10	9	16
Spanish result	5	10	18	20	6	18	16	9	11	6	5	15	11	7	16

The first four results have been plotted on the scatter graph below.

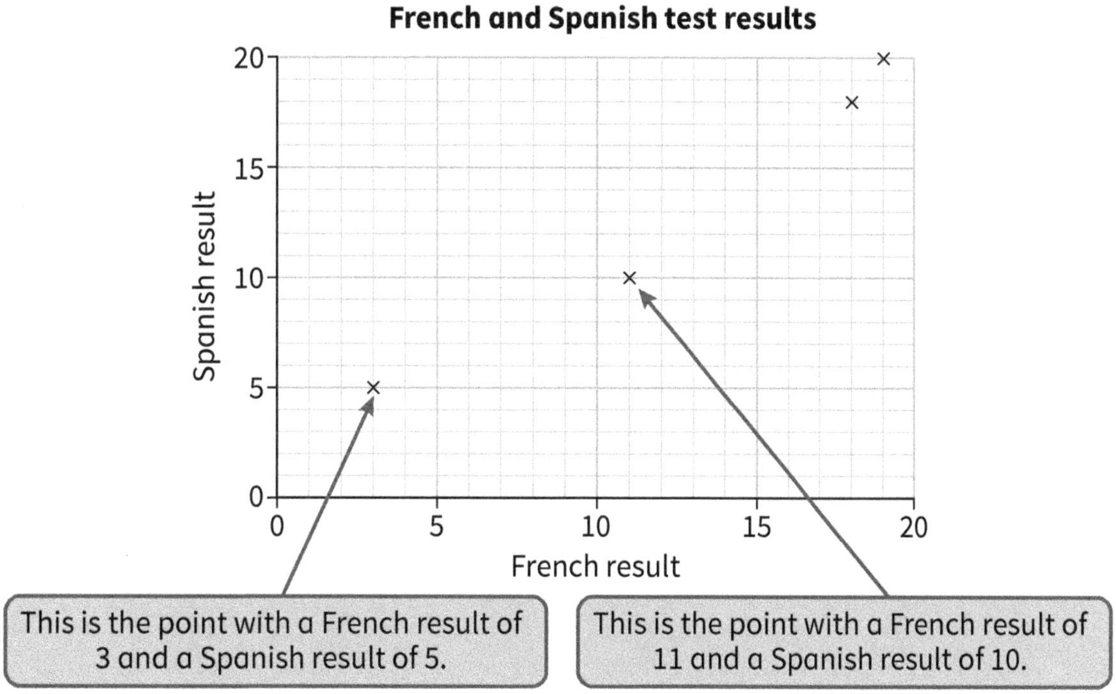

a Plot the remaining points from the table on the scatter graph. Mark each point with a cross. Check you have plotted all the points by counting them. There should be 15 altogether.

b Which of these statements correctly describes the data on the scatter graph? ......

A The better students do in the French test, the better they do in the Spanish test. Also, the worse students do in the French test, the worse they do in the Spanish test.

B The better students do in the French test, the worse they do in the Spanish test. Also, the worse students do in the French test, the better they do in the Spanish test.

This scatter graph is showing a **positive correlation**. This happens when as one value increases, so does the other. In this case, as the French results increase, so do the Spanish results.

2 This table shows the Art and Science test results of 15 students. Each test was marked out of 20.

Art result	3	10	15	8	10	13	4	16	12	8	17	11	5	20	7
Science result	19	11	7	11	10	9	17	5	10	14	2	9	15	4	13

The first three results have been plotted on the scatter graph below.

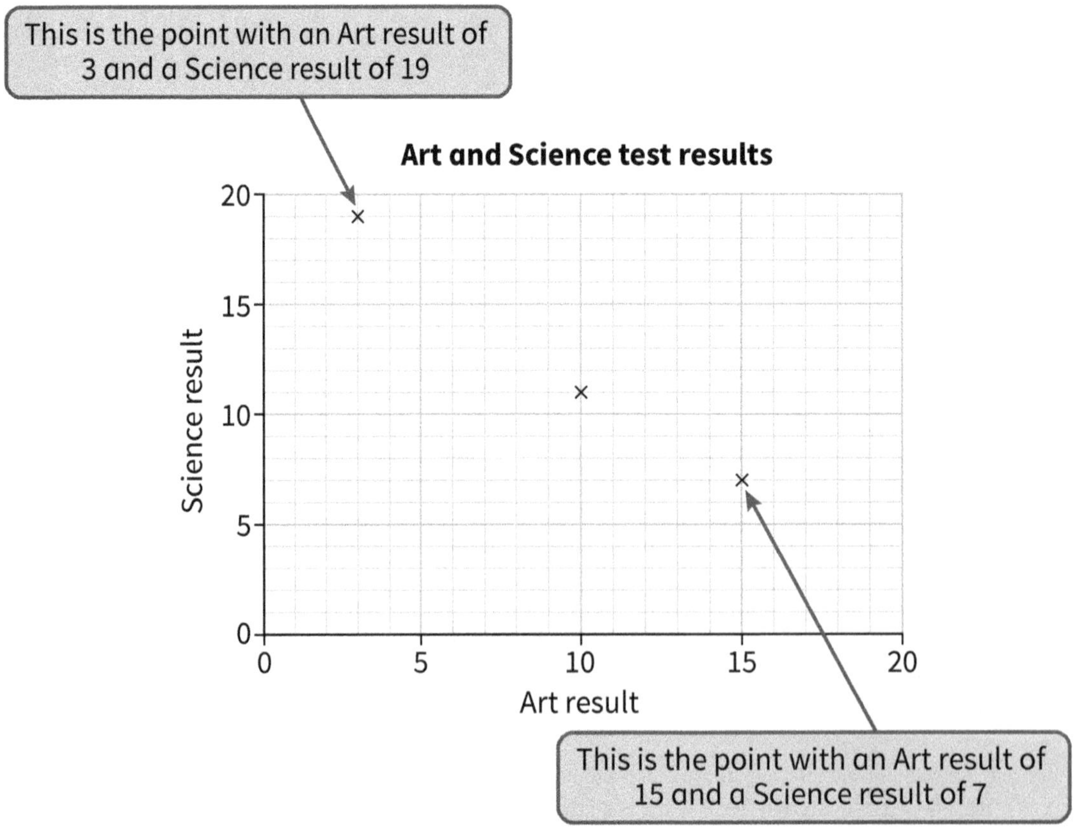

a Plot the remaining points from the table on the scatter graph. Mark each point with a cross.

Check you have plotted all the points by counting them. There should be 15 altogether.

b Which of these statements correctly describes the data on the scatter graph? ......

A The better students do in the Art test, the better they do in the Science test. Also, the worse students do in the Art test, the worse they do in the Science test.

B The better students do in the Art test, the worse they do in the Science test. Also, the worse students do in the Art test, the better they do in the Science test.

This scatter graph is showing a **negative correlation**. This happens when as one value increases, the other decreases. In this case, as the Art results increase, the Science results decrease.

Now try Exercise 19.3 on page 183 of Coursebook 9.

19.4 Interpreting and drawing stem-and-leaf diagrams

A **stem-and-leaf diagram** is a way of showing data in order of size.

1 This table shows the results of a Spanish test taken by the students in class 9R.

Spanish test results for class 9R									
~~15~~	~~14~~	~~26~~	~~16~~	~~5~~	~~22~~	25	10	18	21
22	27	7	23	9	17	20	19	9	24

a Complete the unordered stem-and-leaf diagram below.

The first six entries from the table have been written on the diagram. Cross out the entries from the table as you write them on the diagram.

Key: 0 | 5 means 5

0	|	5		
1	|	5	4	6
2	|	6	2	

The lowest result is 5 and the highest is 27.
So, the stem must have:
0 for the results that are below 10
1 for the results that are between 10 and 19
2 for the results that are between 20 and 29.

b Rewrite the stem-and-leaf diagram above as an ordered stem-and-leaf diagram below.

Key: 0 | 5 means 5

0	|	5	7
1	|	0	4
2	|	0	

You must now write the leaves in order of size in each row of the diagram.

2 This table shows the results of the Spanish test taken by the students in class 9T.

Spanish test results for class 9T									
~~18~~	~~12~~	~~21~~	~~6~~	8	28	4	11	14	21
20	6	17	13	19	28	21	10	12	22

Complete the unordered and ordered stem-and-leaf diagrams below.

Unordered:

Key: 0 | 6 means 6

0	6
1	8 2
2	1

Ordered:

Key: 0 | 4 means 4

0	4 6
1	
2	

3 Combine the two ordered stem-and-leaf diagrams from Questions 1 and 2 to form a back-to-back stem-and-leaf diagram. The first row has been done for you.

Spanish test results for class 9R		**Spanish test results for class 9T**
9 7 5	0	4 6 6 8
	1	
	2	

Key for class 9R: 5 | 0 means 5

Key for class 9T: 0 | 4 means 4

For class 9R copy the leaves from Q1b, but write them in reverse order.

For class 9T copy the leaves from Q2 ordered stem-and-leaf diagram.

Now try Exercise 19.4 on page 185 of Coursebook 9.

Glossary

arithmetic sequence *see* linear sequence

average speed the total distance travelled divided by the total time taken to travel that distance

bearing an angle, measured clockwise from north

column vector two numbers, placed vertically, that describe a translation of a point or shape; the top number gives the number of grid points to move the object along the horizontal axis, the bottom number gives the number of grid points to move the object up or down the vertical axis

cross-section the face formed by slicing through a solid shape

elevation a view of an object from the front or the side

exterior angle an angle formed outside a triangle, or other polygon, between an extended side and the side next to it

factorise write a number or algebraic expression as a product of factors

frequency polygon a chart, made up of straight line segments, that illustrates frequency

gradient (of a line) the gain in height divided by the horizontal distance travelled

index a number used to show a power; in 3^4, 4 is the index

interior angle the angle between two adjacent sides of a polygon that lies inside the polygon

inverse function the function that has the opposite effect; the inverse of the function 'multiply by 2 then add 3' is 'subtract 3 then divide by 2'

linear sequence a sequence of numbers in which the difference between consecutive terms is the same

midpoint the centre point of a line segment

***n*th term** the general term of a sequence; using algebra to write the position-to-term rule, where n represents the position number of the term

order of operations the specific order in which the operations must be done, when carrying out calculations involving more than one operation

plan a view of an object from overhead

Pythagoras' theorem an equation relating the lengths of the sides of a right-angled triangle: the sum of the squares of the two short sides of the triangle is equal to the square of the longest side (or hypotenuse)

regular polygon a polygon in which all the sides are the same length and all the angles are the same size

sample space diagram a diagram that shows all the possible outcomes of an event

scatter graph a graph showing linked values of two variables that may or may not be related, where the data values are plotted as coordinate points

simplest form a fraction in which both the numerator and denominator have been divided by their highest common factor

term-to-term rule a rule to find the next term of a sequence, given the previous term

tessellation a pattern, usually on a flat surface, made up of identically shaped pieces that fit together without overlapping or leaving spaces between them

trial and improvement a method of solving a problem by making repeated guesses